ERNEST BUCKLER REMEMBERED

1st Prize
Dartmouth Book Award
"Non-Fiction", 1990

Claude Bissell

Ernest Buckler *Remembered*

UNIVERSITY OF TORONTO PRESS
Toronto Buffalo London

© University of Toronto Press 1989
Toronto Buffalo London
Printed in Canada

ISBN 0-8020-5814-0

Printed on acid-free paper

Canadian Cataloguing in Publication Data

Bissell, Claude T. (Claude Thomas), 1916–
Ernest Buckler remembered

Bibliography: p.
Includes index.
ISBN 0-8020-5814-0

1. Buckler, Ernest, 1908–   – Biography.
2. Novelists, Canadian (English) – 20th century –
Biography.* I. Title.

PS8503.U2Z57 1989   C813'.54   C89-094285-4
PR9199.3.B82Z57 1989

This book has been published with the help of
the Canada Council and the Ontario Arts Council
under their block grant programs.

Contents

Preface

I first met Ernest Buckler in the summer of 1953. He was then forty-five years old and had just published his first novel, *The Mountain and the Valley*, the previous year. Until his death in 1984, we met almost every year, and we corresponded regularly. I write then about a man whom I knew well and for whom I had great admiration and affection. This book is to a large extent a personal memoir. I have not, however, neglected the essential tools of biography – the examination of correspondence, memoranda, journals, and diaries, and interviews with friends and relatives.

Buckler was a modest man, but he thought of himself as a serious artist, and he kept everything that concerned his work. His personal records (except for some early journals in the 1930s when he was struggling to find himself) are disappointingly slight. But his correspondence is rich and diverse, and constitutes in itself a major literary work. My correspondence with him amounts to some four hundred letters and is a principal source for this book. Many of his close friends have died, but his three sisters – Mona, Olive, and Nelly, all of a ripe age – have reached back in their memories to recall significant details in the life of the brother they adored.

I have described this book as a personal memoir. It is also, in a sense, a family memoir, for Ernest Buckler has often been a subject of delighted family recall. My wife was with me during all the visits to Centrelea, Buckler's home, and she was his companion for much of the time when he spent a month with us in Toronto. My daughter Deirdre has known Ernest since she was a young child, and in recent years she and her husband, Robert Macdonald, have been enthusiastic members of the Buckler circle. My brother Keith used Buckler's words for several of his choral compositions, and greatly admired his work.

A book about Buckler must be primarily about his books. I have not, however, tried, in the fashionable critical manner, to separate the man from his books. I do not believe that each literary text is handed down immaculate on its private Mount Sinai. Buckler did not write specifically autobiographical books (except to a limited extent in *The Mountain and the Valley*). He had read widely in literature and philosophy, and he knew that each book makes its own structural and generic demands. But his books were also his life, and, in a broad sense, they were all autobiographical, his letters to the world.

Buckler was himself a fine critic. He was at his strongest in expressing the peculiar virtues of writers whom he liked. He strove to convey the excitement of his own discoveries and persuade others to follow him. I hope that in some measure I have achieved this same goal.

For the use of the Buckler material in the Public Archives of Nova Scotia I am grateful for permission given by Wayne A. Rice, Buckler's nephew and his executor. Sandra M. Haycock, public records archivist there, extended every courtesy to me during two visits. The staff of the Thomas Fisher Rare Book Library made scholarly research a pleasure. I am most indebted to Mrs Rachel Grover, a Buckler enthusiast, who was responsible for the organization of the Buckler material. She was a constant guide and help in my research.

I am indebted to Mrs Julia Mills of Winchester, Ontario, for several pictures of Ernest during his undergraduate days at Dalhousie. Mrs Mills' father was a cousin of Ernest, and he stayed with the family during his college years, 1924–9. Evelyn Garbary and Margaret Bickley Farmer answered innumerable questions, and gave me permission to use excerpts from their letters.

Without their cooperation my picture of Ernest Buckler would be seriously incomplete. Jocelyn Laurence, for the estate of Margaret Laurence, gave permission for the use of the quotations from her mother's letters to Ernest Buckler. These letters, so typical of Margaret Laurence's warmth and sensitivity, were precious to Buckler. Alistair MacLeod, Alice Munro, and Al Purdy all wrote in praise of Buckler's work, and I am grateful for their permission to use quotations from their letters.

Audrey Douglas prepared a final typewritten version from handwriting that ranges between the difficult and the inscrutable. In the time available to her from full-time obligations, she gave priority to my work, and I am deeply grateful to her.

I acknowledge the help of two editors of the University of Toronto Press: Ian Montagnes (who has guided me through three previous books) urged me to write this book, and Gerry Hallowell gave sympathetic and thoughtful advice during the preparation of the manuscript.

My greatest debt is to Ernest Buckler's three sisters: Mrs Harold Buckler (Nelly), Mrs Raymond Rice (Olive), and Mrs Robert Simpson (Mona). This book is dedicated to them with gratitude and love.

'At the age of twelve after one year at Bridgetown High School, [Ernest, front and centre] completed all requirements for university entrance.'

Buckler with his father, mother, and cousin, Julia Jackson Mills, in the 1920s

'Buckler wrote of [his mother] proudly in a diary that he kept in the thirties that "sophisticated appointments of dress became her amazingly well."' This photo was taken while he was studying mathematics and philosophy at Dalhousie University in Halifax in the 1920s.

'At Dalhousie he was known as the dedicated student. In the Dalhousie Year Book for 1929, he looks out in unsmiling seriousness.'

Ernest and his sister Mona in the early 1930s. 'Mona, closest to him in age, had been his "twin," a relationship tenderly recorded in that between Anne and David in *The Mountain and the Valley*.'

The West Dalhousie Church 'stood on a little rise beside a lake that "lapped softly in the sun, like the breathing of someone asleep."'

'During the summer we made almost yearly visits to Centrelea ... Ernest would be sitting on a chair underneath the chestnut tree, with a book that he had been reading, carefully cultivating, as he said, an air of nonchalance. As our car drew up and he recognized the visitors, he would rise quickly and walk towards the car to greet us.'

'For his work (and his peace of mind), he needed isolation and a particular place ... And the "place" for him was the house in Centrelea.' Photo: courtesy of the Thomas Fisher Rare Book Library, University of Toronto

'Whether we entered by the front or rear door, we would begin with a long session in the kitchen ... The kitchen was the dominating room in the old farmhouse; it was, as Ernest wrote, "thronged with conduciveness."'

Margaret Bickley on graduation from nursing in 1936 some twenty years before she met Ernest.

A recent portrait of Evelyn Bowen Garbary. Photo: Cheryl Lean

Ernest and his oldest sister Nelly at West Dalhousie in the late 1950s. 'Nelly and her husband ... lived in the Buckler house to which Ernest had come at the age of six from the original family house ...'

Ernest and my wife Christine outside his house in 1956

Ernest with Christine and our daughter Deirdre at Port Royal in the early 1960s

Ernest at Port Royal

Ernest in the 1970s

Ernest and I in the early 1980s

'To his great delight, special arrangements were made for an investiture on 16 June 1975 by the governor general, Jules Léger, at the official residence of the Nova Scotia lieutenant governor in Halifax.'

On Saturday, 11 September 1982, we held a reception in Mountain Lea, Bridgetown, with tributes to Buckler and a presentation to commemorate his work. 'Ernest later said that he was sorry Christine and he had no chance to do their Ginger Rogers–Fred Astaire act.'

Ernest and I with Mrs Kaye Hill and Roy McIsaac at the reception

Ernest flanked by his sisters, Olive Rice and Nelly Buckler, after the move to Mountain Lea in 1981

ERNEST BUCKLER REMEMBERED

Life with Ernest

The house where Ernest Buckler lived for the whole of his active life as a writer – a period of almost fifty years – lies a few miles outside Bridgetown, a small town on the north shore of Nova Scotia near the western end of the Annapolis Valley. At the end of a Maritimes motor trip my wife Christine, I, and our daughter Deirdre, aged six, came to the house for the first time on 19 August 1953.

A meeting with Ernest Buckler was one of the reasons for choosing the Maritimes for our first long motor trip; another reason was wartime memories. In the summer of 1942 I had completed my training as an infantry officer, and was waiting in a transit camp near Windsor, Nova Scotia, for a ship to take our draft to England. I was enchanted by the countryside; it had the spaciousness of the ocean that daily surged over the muddy flats of the Avon River. After the war, I had become assistant to the president of the University of Toronto, Sidney Smith, an ardent Maritimer who had accepted exile in western and central Canada as the price of his career. He was particularly insistent that Christine, who had spent her summers in the Hebrides, would not find Ontario lakes a satisfactory substitute for the Atlantic. Now my vivid memory of Nova Scotia scenery and the impact of Sidney Smith's words coalesced with a desire to meet the author of a recent novel of extraordinary beauty and power, *The Mountain and the Valley*.

The desire to meet Buckler was simply a reflex of my admiration for his novel. At that time I was reading a good many Canadian novels in preparation for a yearly survey of Canadian fiction for the *University of Toronto Quarterly*. Between 1947 when my first survey came out and 1952, the year *The Mountain and the Valley* was published, there was much to rejoice in. Morley Callaghan had made a brilliant return to the novel in *The Loved and the Lost*; Hugh MacLennan, Philip Child, and Thomas Raddall strengthened their established positions; two major poets, Earl Birney and Abraham Klein, brought their imaginative scope and verbal brilliance to prose fiction; and there were first novels of an arresting nature by W.O. Mitchell, Henry Kreisel, Ethel Wilson, and Robertson Davies, as well as Ernest Buckler.

In this diverse and splendid setting, *The Mountain and the Valley* had for me a special appeal. It began with a paragraph in which each word seemed to me to be new-minted.

David Canaan had lived in Entremont all his thirty years. As far back as childhood, whenever anger had dishevelled him, or confusion, or the tick, tick, tick, of emptiness like he felt today, he had sought the log road that went to the top of the mountain. As he moved along this road, somewhere the twist of anger would loosen; a shaft of clarity would strike through the scud of confusion; blood would creep back into the pulse and pallor of the emptiness. He would take happiness there, to be alone with it; as another child might keep hidden for a day a toy that wasn't his.

I had the impression that, as Buckler said of Hemingway, 'the printed page almost glittered, as if with sunlight off steel.'[1] In my review I called the novel 'a major work: a full-length novel in which a single vision welds the parts into a whole – in many respects the best novel that has been written in this country.'[2]

Ordinarily, I was reluctant to seek out writers whom I admired, believing this was an intrusion on the private life of the artist. The critical orthodoxy of the day reinforced my academic inhibitions: art existed in splendid isolation from the artists who created it. But, for Buckler, I would make an exception.

He was a new Canadian writer who should be known and celebrated in his own country. Then I hesitated. Perhaps Buckler really wasn't a Canadian writer. *The Mountain and the Valley* had been published by an American firm, Henry Holt, and was dedicated to six men, only one of whom, W.O. Mitchell, was a Canadian. Four of the others – Manuel Komroff, Arnold Gingrich, Louis Paul, Burton Rascoe – were associated with that most American of American magazines, *Esquire*. The little village about which Buckler wrote was not given an immediately recognizable setting and, although the city that loomed in the background was called Halifax, it was not clearly identified. Perhaps Buckler was, like Malcolm Lowry, a Canadian by brief residence with no literary roots in the country, or, like Wallace Stegner, a native Canadian during his early years, but an American during his active literary career. An inquiry to Henry Holt brought the reassuring reply that Buckler lived near a small town in Nova Scotia, close to where he had been born.

I wrote to Buckler, mentioning my review of *The Mountain and the Valley*, and, in the event that he hadn't seen the review, or didn't, as was the proclaimed habit of some writers, read reviews of his own books, I quoted my most enthusiastic comments. He replied in a letter combining an outspokenness with a humorous self-deprecation that cast an anticipatory glow on our meeting.

Indeed I do read reviews of my book. I've always felt that this alleged indifference to what's said about one's work which some writers profess is a thoroughly phony affectation. In fact, by a curious coincidence, I had just written to the *University of Toronto Quarterly* to ask if the book had ever been reviewed there; and if so, if I might have a copy of the review. For one thing, I like to pass such responsible comment on to my American publishers.

Naturally, I was extremely pleased that you liked the book so well. And of course I should like very much to see you when you and your family are passing through these parts – I'm just a country bumpkin (we all are here) and formidable strangers throw me into a vacuous state not unlike that of Mortimer Snerd.

If it's convenient, it might be a good idea to give me a buzz on approach. I live about three miles below Bridgetown, on the post road to Annapolis. Not so much that it would give me a chance to switch from rather aromatic overalls to something a trifle more presentable, as that I could then arrange not to be in the back pasture maybe when you arrive.[3]

We reached Bridgetown early in the afternoon of a mellow August day. We had followed the old road through the Annapolis Valley, which lay serene and golden in late summer ease. We had passed through a succession of small towns, each a sudden flowering on the purposeful highway, the route now flanked by great elms that met overhead, and by houses that, even when big and handsome, did not assert themselves unduly. Bridgetown was such a town. Perhaps there was about it a suggestion of self-satisfaction, a lingering memory of the days when great three-masted ships from Saint John had sailed up the Annapolis River and docked there, or of a more recent past, not altogether vanished, when a thriving industry or two had brought some affluence and a touch of sophistication.

At Bridgetown we phoned to report our arrival and to get detailed instructions about the route we should now follow. We turned south at the main intersection down what was presumably the business street, guarded at each corner by a bank and presided over by a modest town hall, followed the main street across an old iron bridge that spanned the Annapolis River, now a modest stream, until we reached the highway that paralleled the river. We crossed a little creek, known as 'Bloody Creek,' where almost 250 years ago a detachment of British soldiers from Port Royal had been attacked by Indians and a few French, and the water had run red from the blood of the wounded and slain. We now drove slowly watching for the sign, Centrelea, the name of the district where Buckler lived. Shortly after the sign, we spotted the white clapboard house that he had described.

The house was close to the highway, and yet seemed to ignore it, secure in the knowledge that it had existed long before the highway had been put through. A big, umbrageous chestnut tree at the front of the house sealed its privacy. We moved off the highway along a dirt track that skirted the house and came close to a friendly side door. But we instinctively decided that, for a formal first visit, we should use the front door, set between two tall, twelve-paned windows, below the peak of a gable that broke the solid square of the house. The native builders had, in a modest way, tried to follow the formal doorways in the more splendid houses of the era: the door was inset with a transom above, and there was a suggestion on each side of colonettes. The man who answered our knock, however, had no touch of the country squire, even less of the working farmer. He was of middle height, thin, but with a wiry compactness that must have come from vigorous outdoor exercise. The hair was close-cropped with a reddish glint, and the voice was soft and low pitched, with no hint of a Maritime drawl or a rural twang, and the glasses he wore had lenses of scholarly thickness. He wore a blue suit, with shirt and tie. We were suddenly conscious of our casual motoring dress. The suit, we found out later, was Buckler's ceremonial suit, usually worn only at weddings and funerals, but given a special outing for the visit of a distant dignitary.

We were ushered into the living-room that opened up to the left of the central hall. There we were introduced to Buckler's mother, a widow in her late seventies and more robust than her son, with strong features, dominated by a generous nose. She greeted us with warmth, and had a special grandmotherly word for Deirdre. There was clearly a great rapport between mother and son. Buckler wrote of her proudly in a diary that he kept in the thirties that 'sophisticated appointments of dress became her amazingly well and there is about her not the slightest suggestion of the awkwardness that country people cannot help showing when they encounter the unaccustomed, whether in dress, environment or company.'[4]

Mrs Buckler presided with easy formality over a generous tea. The conversation moved smoothly. We talked about our delight in the Maritimes, and the Bucklers responded happily with reminiscences. I reiterated my admiration for *The Mountain and the Valley*, and Buckler thanked me for my review and talked in general about the setting of the novel, which he explained was a synthesis of various spots in the valley. Tea finished, Buckler suggested we take a short walk. We paused to watch a pig in a pen – so far the only clear indication that Buckler was an active farmer. Buckler tossed a round, juicy apple into the trough, 'and we watched his money lender eyes above the flat button snout with the two thread-holes in it go nearly mellow as he scrabbled up the apple and maneuvered it between his jaws for the first voluptuous, splitting crunch.'5 We walked through fields that stretched down to the Annapolis River and had been cleared of the hay now stored in a barn across the highway.

It was now almost five, and we had planned to spend our final night in Nova Scotia in Sandy Cove before taking the Digby ferry. We explained this, and said our farewells. Sandy Cove is a famous summer retreat that friends had celebrated. It was well over an hour's drive to the west along a thin peninsula that stretched into the Bay of Fundy, and, having no booking, we were anxious to get there before sundown. But preliminary inquiries about overnight accommodation were not promising. This, we concluded, was a haven for old habitués, not a place for the casual motorist. Then, as gloom thickened at the prospect of no haven for the night, Christine had a sudden idea. Why not return to the motel a mile or so from the Buckler house that had advertised vacancies, and then phone the Bucklers and suggest a second visit. I warmly concurred. Together we had felt a kinship with the Bucklers. But we had just cracked the carapace of formality, and we sensed that another and more spontaneous meeting might complete the process. Had we not made that second visit, out meeting with Ernest Buckler would in all likelihood have resulted in a polite thank you note and a continuing but remote interest in his literary career. Our second visit was the beginning of a thirty-year friendship that became central in our lives.

Around 8:00 p.m. we reached our Centrelea Motel, and telephoned Buckler to ask if he and his mother could stand a second visit. There was no doubt about his response. They would be pleased to see us again, and his voice carried conviction. This, as I found out later, was unusual, since on the telephone his voice usually trailed off into a dull, slightly minatory monotone. Would we, he asked, delay our second visit for about an hour until he had made a few arrangements? When we arrived shortly after 9:00 p.m. the 'arrangements' had been made. Tea had been replaced by a bottle of gin, and a young lady, who was clearly on friendly terms with the Bucklers, joined in the reception. She was introduced as Diana Lockhart, a librarian in Annapolis Royal. One of her responsibilities was the bookmobile, which provided a service to the surrounding countryside, and Buckler was the star customer, whose appetite for books was both prodigious and exotic, anything Miss Lockhart told us, from Sophocles to Mailer. In a letter, Buckler sang her praises: 'The Bookmobile is under the direction of Miss Diana Lockhart: a Varsity graduate, and one of the most personable, knowledgeable, humorous, perceptive young ladies extant. She seems to sense with an almost radio-like telepathy exactly what books each person will like.'[6] Buckler had now discarded his best suit for an open shirt, casual trousers, and sneakers. His mother ceased to be the hostess presiding at the tea-table, and joined heartily in the merry talk and modestly in the consumption of the gin. The hours rolled by. Deirdre was put to sleep in an upstairs bedroom, and all thoughts of Sandy Cove and its charms faded.

Memory rescues from the evening a few recurring subjects. One was the comedies of country life, even when the stage was such a beautiful and historic town as Annapolis Royal. The particular event for discussion was the annual celebration known as Natal Day. Buckler, who hadn't been at a celebration for many years, viewed it as low comedy. 'There would have been,' he declared, 'a procession of tawdry crepe paper floats enthroning a Miss Blueberry and a Miss Black Currant and a Miss Iceberg Lettuce, and "Athaletes" running and jumping over things, and in the hallowed Fort grounds slatterny picnic mothers shouting to their chocolate-smeared children: "Now you come right back here, do you hear? If you don't I'll smack your ass but good." ' Diana Lockhart contributed an element of black comedy to the scene: she remembered an incident when a stallion, unwisely admitted to the parade, had an amorous encounter with a mare also in the parade, with resultant chaos and embarrassment.

We turned inevitably to the Canadian reception of *The Mountain and the Valley*. It had been published to wide critical acclaim in the United States and had sold reasonably well there, but the Canadian agent, Clarke, Irwin, had ordered only a few copies for the Canadian market and had given it little promotion. But word spread fast in the Annapolis Valley that a local man had written about the valley and that he had failed to render fully the nobility and sophistication of local life. Moreover, he had unduly emphasized the bodily functions, and, worst of all, had written about sex with a lewd relish. Buckler reported that it was often the very type whose own sexual life was untidy who took exception to the book's frankness. He reported with delight the unexpected response of a local Anglican cleric to a parishioner who complained about the book: 'I said to her, it seems to me that if I thought such and such things shouldn't be written about and I'd known that this book dealt with those things, as you did, I simply shouldn't have read it. But it seems to me that you were very eager to read it.' Mrs Buckler entered the discussion spiritedly. 'Some of those folks who complain about Ern's book had better take another good look at the Bible. There are lots of good, spicy stories in it.'

When we left at 3:00 a.m. with Deirdre, half asleep and bundled into a blanket, we said our farewells to Mrs Buckler and Ernest. We knew that a fresh and fascinating chapter had begun. After Ernest's death thirty years later I came across the entry for 19 August 1953 in a laconic diary that he kept at the time. It read: 'Bissells arrived in the afternoon. Tea, goodbys, then returned for the evening. Di here. Really a marvellous evening.'

After this first meeting, we wrote to each other regularly. The arrival of a letter from Ernest was a major family event.

The envelopes could be recognized easily by the distinctive signature of the old upright typewriter he used, or, now and then, by the clear handwriting with occasional circular flourishes, and the letters would be a composition, never a miscellany of facts and polite inquiries. The letters brimmed with life, because they were written carefully, with the full resources of the man and the artist. Indeed he used to joke that it often took him the better part of the morning to write a note to the milkman.

Often the letter had a *New Yorker*ish glint. There would be annotated quotations from the local newspapers. He noticed a story that the police inspector had fined a man 'for having insufficient equipment,' and the locals were now, he reported, quaking in their shorts. The meetings of the women's auxiliary was a rich source for quotations. Roll call, he reported, was answered in a variety of imperious ways, for instance, by each member giving a fact about Venezuela, or, more demandingly, by reading a verse from the Bible containing the word 'persecution.' In the midst of a solemn critical appraisal – of a book on University College, University of Toronto, that I had edited, whose dust cover reproduced the college crest with its motto *Parum Claris Lucem Dare*, to give light wherever light is needed – he inserted this comic gambit:

Di and I had an awful wrestle with the motto *Parum Claris Lucem Dare* ... As a challenge to our decrepit Latin we set about quite seriously at first pairing noun and adjective according to case, gender, etc. ... and then, in one of her wildly tangential (though often inspired) absurdities, Di proposed: 'I dare ya to throw a little clear light around here!' I countered with 'I dare ya to parboil Clare Luce.'[7]

A domestic scene would inspire a marvellous word cartoon:

How was Christmas with you? Mine was very lonesome until the afternoon of Christmas Day when a sister and her husband arrived, bringing with them four children, a dog, Johnny Walker, and two charming long-necked characters from Heidseick & Co. From then on things certainly accelerated. Most arrivals take a little while to build up steam. But that aggregation blossoms into pandemonium the minute they set foot into the kitchen. In a matter of seconds, there were tracks laid around the dining room table, cars going hell for leather on them, the dog was chasing our cat, skates were knee-deep on the parlor floor (though there wasn't a skim of ice in sight), the youngest was dragging an undrawn turkey like a yule log down the long hall, and the babel! 'Grammie, look what I got' 'Brian, will you please not eat any more candy today!' (By this time, licked-over creams were a real hazard to navigation and little rivulets of pop from akimbo-held bottles had begun to delta the whole place.) 'Mummy, I gotta pee!' 'Daddy, where's my wires for the remote control cars?' 'I told you that was your responsibility, that you were to see they went in.' 'I want the wires for my remote control cars!' 'Mummy, Barry won't let me in the bathroom!' 'Where's the baby?' 'My soul, he isn't outside (he was) without anything on, is he?' 'Oh, don't go near that rickety old plant stand, dear. If it fell over that old plant would cut your little head open.' 'Ernie, I got *this*.' 'Mummy, I gotta pee!' *'Where's the baby?'* ... It was pandemonium but every minute was wonderful. Somehow I got a chance to read *The Ponder Heart*. (Eudora Welty's latest) to the really exceptional eldest one I was, I think, speaking to you about when you were here – the one with the really frightening imagination and the defiant but infinitely vulnerable and sort of lost-eyed face that breaks my heart. He was enchanted with it.[8]

He wrote about the books he was reading – modern fiction, poetry, and criticism chiefly – an early letter reports that 'Di feeds me Kafka and Cyril Connolly in such doses as she feels I can take. Firbank, though, I brought right up again.'[9] In the course of our correspondence, he referred to almost every significant contemporary novelist, usually with a distinctive and illuminating comment. When he was working on a book and felt confident, even if only tentatively, about its outcome, the letter would become a writer's diary. And at times, more often as the years went by, a melancholy bred by isolation and increasing bad health would creep in. It appears even in some of the early letters that are usually gay and sunlit. It was two years after our first meeting that he wrote:

Nova Scotia is very beautiful now. In a lonesome kind of way. A couple of weeks ago they fished one of my few only friends here out of the river, drowned as drowned. Cruel the sun. Cruel the grass dreaming in the fields. Cruel the June. One summer we had three grand people come to see us. That doesn't happen any more.[10]

For some time a second visit was not easy to arrange. Bridgetown was 1200 miles from Toronto. The flight to Halifax could be swift (barring fog), but there followed at least another three hours by rail, bus, or rented car. It was expensive and difficult to squeeze into a time-table now crammed with teaching, administration, and official travel that could absorb much of the summer. It was not likely that Ernest would come to Toronto even if he had the time and the money. His house and a small area around it were his kingdom, and he had no intention of leaving it. We finally made it to Bridgetown in 1956. Three years of exchanging letters had developed an easy intimacy and, when we met again, we felt that we had just parted. By 1960 the problem of distance had been solved. Christine and I had completed the purchase and renovation of a farmhouse in Cape Breton where we planned to spend most of our summers. Bridgetown was 350 miles away, and it was not difficult to make a side-trip. We hoped that occasionally Ernest would find it possible to visit us in Cape Breton, especially as he had never seen it. But he persistently resisted our pleas. He had – or pretended that he had – a fixed idea of cocktail parties given by sophisticated summer residents in which the talk had a Noel Cowardish brittleness, or of leisurely strolls in white flannel trousers on a mermaid-haunted beach. The reality, we assured him, was a simple rural existence as uneventful as his own, but he chose not to believe us.

During the summer we made almost yearly visits to Centrelea, supplemented in later years by visits in the spring that I made by myself. The summer visits gradually developed a plot that varied from year to year only in detail. At first, we planned to arrive in Centrelea on the day we left Cape Breton, which meant a late arrival after dusk, or as it was falling. Ernest would be sitting on a chair underneath the chestnut tree, with a book that he had been reading, carefully cultivating, as he said, an air of nonchalance. As our car drew up and he recognized the visitors, he would rise quickly and walk towards the car to greet us. In later years, we would take a more leisurely approach and break our trip with an overnight stay at Chester. Now our arrival time was not fixed, and we would designate it as sometime in the afternoon. On these occasions, Ernest would remain inside and, when he heard the car, would bound out the kitchen door to meet us. Greetings and farewells were always deeply emotional moments for him. 'When you go out to welcome someone,' he wrote in *The Cruelest Month*, 'the ground seems to rise up to meet your feet' but 'the moment of leaving seemed shot with treason.'[11]

Whether we entered by the front or rear door, we would begin with a long session in the kitchen, like diplomats first exchanging confidences with the head of a friendly state in his private quarters. The kitchen was the dominating room in the old farmhouse; it was, as Ernest wrote, 'thronged with conduciveness.'[12] At Centrelea, it no longer served its original functions, as a resting place for the men returning from the fields, as an evening schoolroom for the children, or as the perimeter of the woman's whole life. A bachelor and a writer had different needs, but these needs could still be satisfied in the old environment. 'The table was still queen of the room, as the stove was still king,'[13] but one was now a place for books and magazines (as was the couch), and the other, especially on cool days or after the sun had set, the presiding spirit of the room.

In the evening, after dinner, we moved to the living-room, the room where we had had our first meeting. At one side was an upright piano that served chiefly as a display for photographs, the most prominent a picture of Ernest's mother. The low table in front of the divan was piled with past issues of magazines, chiefly of *Esquire*, whose dominance was initially a puzzle until

I learned more about Ernest's début as a writer. I recall a television set that functioned during our early visits, then declined
and fell silent and pictureless. Towards the end of the sixties
it was succeeded by a hi-fi, a gift from Ernest's friend, Evelyn
Garbary. It remained in separate pieces, interspersed with little
mounds of records. Ernest said that he was intimidated by the
hi-fi. 'I just press buttons hit or miss, and all that happens is
that things start lifting and dipping and gliding and revolving
and the great spectral arm waves around but never in the direction to play and the speakers crackle like incipient volca-
noes ... so that I just yank the master plug and flee for my life,
with Flagstad and Callas untapped, to the kitchen.'[14] I doubted
whether he ever mastered it, for as soon as a record session
began I was promptly designated engineer and producer. At
every visit, I would spend a good deal of time searching for the
cut of the 'Liebestod' in the recording of *Tristan and Isolde*. It
was his favourite, and as the music moved to its surging climax,
he would often retire in tears. He accumulated a considerable
collection of records through the years – all, I think, the gift of
friends who knew his tastes. Our division was drama, and, over
the years, our Christmas present was always a record: classical
dramas like *Othello*, *Hamlet*, some Greek tragedies, *The Importance of Being Ernest*, *Love for Love*, *Hedda Gabler*, contemporary plays such as Albee's *A Delicate Balance*, Tennessee
Williams' *The Glass Menagerie* (a great favourite), and Samuel
Beckett's *Chairs*, a selection of one-act plays by Yeats, Simon
Gray's *Butley*, Robert Lowell's *Benito Cerino*, and *The Old
Glory*, an anthology of Brechtian monologues. There were many
records of Leontyne Price, whom he adored, and of opera excerpts, chiefly of Verdi.

His record collection – other friends added to it over the years
– was precious to him. 'I'm always captured by the mystery,'
he wrote to me, 'of what words to be spoken or laughs to be
laughed, or tears to be shed are holding their breaths in those
miniscule grooves of the platters.'[15] Ernest also had a collection
of popular records of the thirties and forties, and, late in the
evening, he and Christine would put on what he styled their

Fred Astaire–Ginger Rogers act. He danced with deftness and with great brio – a legacy from Dalhousie days when, he recalled, he and Janet MacNeill (later Janet Piers), a daughter of his favourite professor, were 'The Charleston wizards.'

On the other side of the broad central hall – 'a cool throat that brought in the poplared or the daisied September breeze'[16] – was the parlour, which we entered only as observers. It contained an old organ with 'mice proof' pedals, a sewing-machine, a Morris chair, a wicker rocker, a settee with a cluster of grapes on its back, and the one stylish picture in the house – an old lithograph that was the artist's distillation of an exotic European landscape – dark and mysterious, a sombre lake with a gondola-like vessel poised in its centre and a stag standing on the shore. The room's chief use was as an overflow for Ernest's records and books. This 'mausolenic' room came alive once when my brother Keith, working on a musical setting of Ernest's prose meditation on Christmas, used the organ to provide the orchestral setting for the narration.

To the rear of the parlour was a room that, whatever its original function, was now Ernest's study. It had a simple desk dominated by an old upright typewriter, and a sofa on which manuscripts and correspondence were neatly arranged. Ernest maintained that he had no coherent filing system, but, when the University of Toronto subsequently bought his papers, he quickly produced from the cramped attic and from various containers strewn throughout the house a formidable collection of correspondence, manuscripts, and magazine and newspaper cuttings that went back to his earliest literary efforts.

We had our meals in the dining-room. It was a good-sized room. The main pieces of furniture, a dining-room table and a sideboard, had a solid, substantial quality to them. The sideboard held the domestic treasures – the butter dish with the cut-glass dome, the fragile old cups, the cake platter with the flower patterns. Against the window, on a wooden dais, an aspidistra spread refulgently. Scattered on the floor against the walls were little pyramids of books, borrowed from the bookmobile or publishers' copies (Ernest boasted that he never had to buy a book).

Ernest had no interest in cooking and very little in eating, and during early visits Christine took over the kitchen. During later visits, the table would be set gleamingly, and the refrigerator in the pantry adjoining the kitchen would be packed with a roasted chicken or turkey, a meat loaf, a large bowl of scalloped potatoes, an apple pie, strawberry shortcake, all the work of Nelly and Olive, Ernest's two married sisters who lived nearby, and Olive's husband, Raymond, who was a professional chef.

Upstairs, reached by a broad, commanding staircase that rose gently from the hall a few feet from the front door, were four good-sized bedrooms. Here the sense of gentility vanished. The entire floor was covered with the 'glass-eyed horror of linoleum,'[17] and the pale unfestive wallpaper on the walls reinforced the impression. But the bedroom furniture of solid, old Nova Scotian craftsmanship softened the initial effect. The master bedroom, which we were assigned, Ernest called the Stephen Foster room, because it was 'acutely reminiscent of the one they found Stephen Foster dying in, drunk and penniless'[18] – one of his amusing fantasies of self-denigration.

The pattern for the two- or three-day visit varied little from year to year. Ernest would have preferred, I am sure, not to stir from the house, and to carry on a perpetual symposium, punctuated by food, drink, drama, and music. He liked a limerick that I wrote after one of our visits:

> Although the setting is faintly East Lynne,
> There are lashings and lashings of gin.
> I fear Lord Tennyson
> Would not give his benison
> To the strange talk of love, hate, and sin.

He professed to be reluctant to send us out on the road, since, he said, we had already travelled far and had much farther to go. For a few years following the sudden (but still miserably

low) increase in his income from *The Mountain and the Valley*
royalties, he had owned a car. His decision to sell it was not
only a financial necessity, but a blessed relief to himself and
his neighbours. He was an uncertain and nervous driver, reasonably comfortable on a straight highway, but wayward and
unpredictable when faced by sudden curves, thickening traffic,
or the necessity to turn around. He had, moreover, no desire
to be a Baedeker, although he knew the history of the area well.
He was proud of the reconstruction of Champlain's early sev-
enteenth-century 'habitation' at Port Royal, and occasionally
in his books he makes us aware that his simple rural community had links, through four centuries, with Europe. He went
with us to Port Royal on a number of occasions, and we felt
the force of some early words he had written.

If you stand on the cannon platform on an Indian-summer, still afternoon with a fly buzzing idly in the leaded parchment windows behind
you and look out over the sleeping-stillwaters of the Annapolis Basin
where so much Canadian history was made and over the Sunday-still
villages that border it, you do get the feeling that, in this spot, time
itself has been enclosed and arrested – and that if you turned quickly
enough you might catch a glimpse of Champlain or Lescarbot himself.[19]

This early passage became in *Window on the Sea* a concentrated
poetic statement: ' ... The everlasting shudder of time in Port
Royal (where North America started ...) '
    Ernest wrote about Bridgetown in an early article entitled
'First Stop before Paradise.'[20] (Paradise was the hamlet a mile
or so to the east of Bridgetown.) The article began as affectionate
reminiscences in the manner of Leacock in *Sunshine Sketches
of a Little Town*, but ended with a touch of native boosterism:
'our "ordinary" High school has turned out three Rhodes schol-
ars.' Bridgetown, he wrote, produces not just amiable eccen-
trics. Its odd characters often turn out to have sophisticated
literary tastes similar to Buckler's. He was able to borrow Elizabeth Bowen's *The Heat of the Day* from a garage mechanic,
and he once surprised a retired farmer reading Henry James.

But during our thirty years of acquaintance, he rarely spoke about Bridgetown, and certainly never encouraged us to explore it. Indeed, Bridgetown remained a static backdrop on the last stage of our trip to Centrelea until in later years we stayed at a town motel and were invited by the mayor, Roy McIsaac, a Buckler enthusiast, to join some of the local worthies in their daily coffee sessions. His declining interest in Bridgetown fitted into a theory he developed about town society as a wasteland between rural simplicity and urban sophistication. In *The Mountain and the Valley*, David despised most of the town people:

They didn't seem like people it would be possible to know, or to be known by. They lacked the rich soil of his neighbours' original simplicity. They lacked too the rich soil of those people in the city who had gone beyond this artificial complexity of theirs to simplicity again ... The town people seemed to have only a thin personal topsoil. Nothing grew on it but a sparse crop of self-assurance. They were absolutely unresponsive to anything outside their own narrow communion.[21]

Even Annapolis Royal came under the general condemnation. In *The Cruelest Month*, Annapolis, or Granfort, its fictional name, which is 'town' to the guests at the rural retreat, is not the long royal entrance that motorists recall but a dingy back street where vulgarity and conformism rule.

There was one place in the valley that escaped the slightest suggestion of Ernest's disparagement. It was so deeply attached to his imaginative life that it became almost holy to him. Indeed it was only after we had known him many years that he took us to this special place. We had gone several times to West Dalhousie, a few miles to the south of Bridgetown. His oldest sister, Nelly, and her husband (also a Buckler, but not related) lived in the Buckler house to which Ernest had come at the age of six from the original family house, nearby but long since demolished. At the time I had assumed that this was Entremont of *The Mountain and the Valley*, or Norstead, as it was called in *Ox Bells and Fireflies*. But the community of which he wrote had been to the west of the present village and had long since disappeared. Along the narrow dirt road there had been, for a distance of about four miles, a succession of substantial houses built by the first settlers. The farms went back narrowly from the road to heavily wooded hills, so that families were not far apart and formed a community. After the First World War, lumber companies had offered tempting sums for timber, and, when the owners moved to nearby towns on the strength of what seemed like life-time security, the houses were abandoned and left to decay. To the uninstructed visitor there remained no sign of the old community. Bushes and young trees crowded the edge of the road, and a deep hush hung over the countryside. Ernest pointed out sites of houses, but they were invisible to us. We passed a small stream that flowed under the road. A short distance away, Ernest said, the stream had swelled into a pool, the baptismal pool of *The Mountain and the Valley*, where the young boys had gathered to swim and disport themselves. He retold the story in *Ox Bells and Fireflies* of how a group of chattering boys had watched a baptizing ceremony from one side of the pool, and had aroused the ire of the officiating Baptist clergyman. He had shaken his fist at them and, while the candidate's head was still under water, had shouted, 'I'll do the talking over here.'

One building of the dead community had been preserved. That was the Anglican church, at the southern end of the community. It stood on a little rise beside a lake that 'lapped softly in the sun, like the breathing of someone asleep.'[22] It was a wooden church, with a modest steeple. Inside it was barren of all ornament. The pulpit had been hewn from native wood, and the sides were finished with tongue-and-groove boarding. While we were inspecting the church, a man arrived (Ernest recognized him as an old member of the community) and said that he was in charge of preparations for an annual service that reunited many of the old parishioners. (His chief problem was to eliminate the bats, and he reported on an effective agent – rags soaked in embalming fluid.)

Ernest was an Anglican by family inheritance, reinforced by aesthetic preference. After attending a service at 'the old home church,' as the West Dalhousie Church was called, he wrote, 'the dignified litany of the Church of England and its severely corseted hymns are rather beautiful.' But the holy place for him in this long-vanished community was not the church, but the cemetery that nestled against it. There his parents and grandparents were buried, and there he was to join them. The cemetery became a touchstone in his imaginative life, a place where life and death intersected peacefully and consolingly. 'Yet there was no gloom about the place; only a gentle steeping together of the quiet and the sun and the lake. The black granite stone was warm as flesh to the touch.'[23]

When we left the church and continued southward, the road soon mounted sharply, and great rocks, like rough sculptures, lined each side. 'There,' said Ernest, 'was the boundary between us and another community. Like ours it has disappeared in the wilderness.'

There were few visitors during our days at Centrelea. Occasionally a neighbour or a relative would drop in and Ernest would greet them in a friendly way. He was meticulous about replying to letters about his own work, especially if they came from students, but to unheralded, gushing visitors he could deliver an icy snub. He recalled the lady who, as soon as he opened the door, exclaimed, 'Oh! that must be the mountain,' pointing to the north mountain several miles away, 'and this is the valley,' encompassing the surrounding fields with a sweep of her arm. He had special friends in the area who shared his interests, relished his humour, and were admirers of his work. One was Tom Forrestall, the artist, whose 'magic realism' paintings Ernest admired, perhaps because the luminous detail in Forrestall's scenes of country life rendered in paint what Ernest rendered in words. Forrestall had been born in the area and spent his summers in a small village a few miles away. Ernest speculated about taking us to see him. 'He's a big one,' he said, 'a hell of a good "natural" guy.' But he never quite reached a decision about a visit. We never met another cherished friend, Roy Laurence, a lawyer in Annapolis Royal, a Cape Bretoner by birth, who had, said Ernest, the native Cape Bretoner's relish for stories, sharpened by a sophisticated wit. To Roy Laurence's wife, Mona, like her husband a great favourite, Ernest wrote on 6 November 1976: 'and Mona, what fun we've always had together, haven't we. I remember that many, many nights when I was feeling depressed almost to speechlessness and suddenly you and Roy would come into the kitchen with bounce and smiles and at once the "weather" of my mind would turn to sheer enjoyment.'

One of Ernest's local friends we met by accident. We (myself, Christine, our daughter Deirdre, now in her late twenties, and her husband, Robert Macdonald) had gone to Bridgetown to do some shopping. Ernest, as usual, showed no interest in going. We returned to find him sitting on the kitchen couch, quietly smoking a cigarette, with blood streaming down his face and a trail of blood leading across the kitchen and into the pantry. Our first thought was that an assailant had burst in and attacked him. But Ernest explained that he had fallen in the pantry and cut himself on the edge of a tin. He protested that he was fine and no action was called for. Christine and Deirdre ignored his protestations and sprang into action. Deirdre phoned Gordon Mahaney in Bridgetown, who, we knew, was Ernest's doctor. Christine washed the blood off Ernest's face, and saw immediately that there was a long cut on his forehead. Ernest still protested that all was well, and gently resisted our attempts to escort him to the car. He finally consented to go and smiled wanly when someone observed that, with the large towel wrapped around his head, he looked like an Indian potentate.

Dr Mahaney was a celebrated character in the district, famed for his swiftness and sureness in diagnosis, and for having presided at the birth of several generations of locals. He lived in a big house on the main street which also contained his surgery with its separate entrance. In our excited state we knocked on the door to the private residence. Mrs Mahaney appeared and exclaimed, 'My God Ernie, what have you done now?' Before taking him to the surgery, she invited us into the living-room.

Then she added, 'You all look a little stunned. Sit down, and I'll get you all a drink. I must go and help my husband.' Some time later, patient, doctor, and assistant emerged with a bandaged Ernest. We adjourned outside to the patio for a modest celebration. Ernest, solemn and looking a little repentant at what he later described as his 'Grand Guignol' performance, reached for a drink, but was sternly admonished by the doctor that this was not a sound post-operative procedure. As we left, Mrs Mahaney (whom we subsequently knew as Dot) presented us with six freshly boiled lobsters. We returned praising the Mahaneys. Christine speculated: 'Where else could you take a patient to a doctor, be received by his wife and invited into the living-room, given a drink, and then after the patient was swiftly and surely dealt with, sent off with a half dozen lobsters.'

Ernest finally took us to see one of his 'local' friends. This was Arthur Kennedy, the actor, who had a summer place just below Annapolis Royal, a big, remodelled farmhouse furnished with thoughtful opulence. Behind the house, stretching up a hillside, was a corral, where delicate Arabian horses pastured, and, above this, were a series of ponds created from marshes. It was a strange hobby, I thought, but perhaps a suitably grand one for an artist of international stature. The occasion for meeting Kennedy and his charming wife was a reception they held for local residents, a group tending towards retired admirals, elderly widows, and brisk young businessmen from Montreal and Halifax who were members of the local summer squirearchy. Ernest was nervous about meeting company of this kind, and had prepared for the occasion with a few drinks, which left him tottery and prone to indiscretion. After the formal party, however, he rapidly recovered. We were invited by the Kennedys to remain, and we adjourned to the spacious old kitchen for food and drink, and less inhibited talk.

We had seen Arthur Kennedy a few years before on Broadway where he had a principal role in Arthur Miller's new play, *The Price*, and Ernest had reminded us that Kennedy had had a long association with Miller, having played in the first productions of *All My Sons*, *Death of a Salesman* (in which he played 'Biff'), and *The Crucible*. Ernest delighted in describing Kennedy's continuous international itinerary – to Sicily to make a film, back in New York for some bread-and-butter voice-overs, a sojourn in Palm Beach, then to Rome for another picture. But Kennedy had nothing about him of the self-satisfied performer living on adulation. He was a broad-shouldered, sandy-haired man who wore horn-rimmed glasses and spoke with a deep, resonant voice that commanded any situation. Ernest wrote about him: ' ... you have such "presence" ... that it fills any room you're in (right down to the hidden corners or behind the divans) and so magnifies your burly physical self even (to ten times the poundage it would elicit from any ordinary humdrum scales) that there's hardly room for anyone else,'[24] and the 'presence' was deepened by his wide knowledge of literature and his critical sharpness. Certainly it was not decreased in the eyes of Ernest by his admiration for *The Mountain and the Valley*. 'He has given me enormous encouragement,' said Ernest, 'and plugged my wares from here to Dietrich.'

During the evening we turned to the subject of acting, led for obvious reasons by Kennedy. The work of Kate Reid, who had appeared in *The Price* with Kennedy, came up for discussion. Ernest was a devout (although not uncritical) worshipper. Her 'repetitive mannerisms,' he said, often become beguiling virtues: 'Throwing her head abruptly back and then as abruptly forward and talking (in that induplicable half-haughty, half-raucous, half-lady, half-whore voice) out of, so to speak, those gorgeous, transforming, fathomless eyes.'[25]

I have said that Ernest always resisted invitations to come to Cape Breton or Toronto. But there was one extraordinary exception to what we had sadly concluded was an inflexible resolve. In the fall of 1964 he came to Toronto and stayed with us for an unimaginable month. At that time I was president of University of Toronto, and hence we were living in the president's house, a large and impressive residence centrally located in Rosedale. It was his only absence from Centrelea during the period we knew him, except for an enforced trip to the Lahey Clinic in Boston in his later years. It happened this way.

The CBC, which had done a radio version of *The Mountain and the Valley*, was seriously considering a television version. (There was some talk of Raymond Massey playing the father – a lean, craggy, Maritimes Lincoln.) They asked Ernest to come to Toronto for consultations. Ernest explained in a letter that he would stay at a hotel, courtesy the CBC, and then get in touch with us. Then he went on to say: 'I honestly worry about the stupid company I would be, paralyzed, near-speechless as this country mouse is by the prospect of breasting the city again.'[26] On the completion of his official business, we could imagine his voice on the telephone pitched in a solemn key, stolidly reciting the old ritual that made an extended visit impossible – an expiring furnace, an immediate deadline for a difficult book review, or one of his many ailments. We resolved on strong but benign measures. On Saturday, 12 September, the day his CBC responsibilities ceased, we had reservations for a revue at a dinner theatre near Ernest's hotel. At the end of the performance we walked over to the hotel and knocked on his door. He appeared in his dressing gown, having just arisen from his bed. Christine quietly informed him that he was coming with us (the CBC would be informed of his departure), and she began to pack his valise. His polite protestations gradually ceased, and he went with us resignedly.

The following morning he took up his usual stance. He must leave soon. The book review was for the *New York Times*. He didn't want to jeopardize his association with the newspaper, which brought him some recognition in the American literary world and supplemented his meagre income from royalties. I knew that reviewing for him meant a major effort, in which he gradually reduced an extended critical summary to a concentrated, allusive essay of a prescribed few hundred words. I told him he could have my study on the third floor, which I never used during the day. When he saw the study – a large room with a spacious desk, the whole area insulated from the rest of the house – he began to soften. He had brought along the book to be reviewed, Frank Swinnerton's novel *Quadrille*, with his marginal comments, and perhaps such a small effort did not require the familiar environment of his own house. He agreed to give it a try. Christine had to be away from the house during the day and had warned him that our Italian cleaning woman would be arriving shortly, and that she spoke little English. In the evening when we both returned, Ernest reported that the review was going well. Asunta had come to the study, and greeted him in Italian. He replied with the few Italian words he knew, and she withdrew bowing and smiling. 'It was like a farewell scene in a Verdi opera,' he said. And the relaxed witticism was a good omen. He phoned his sister, who urged him to stay on as long as he liked; the house, she assured him, would be well looked after. His defences had now crumbled, and he faced the rigours of city life with a good heart.

Two incidents stand out in the Toronto visit. One evening, towards the end of September, with a wintery nip in the air, Christine and Ernest bundled themselves up unfashionably and, along with Zephyr, our big thoughtful poodle, set out to visit Walter Bowen, a young lawyer and a relative of mine, who had been a member of our household during his law school days. Walter and a fellow lawyer, Lionel Feldman, had established themselves in a coach-house attached to a big Rosedale residence. That evening Walter and Lionel were entertaining to dinner a distinguished member of the University of Toronto Law School, Edward McWhinney, and his wife, and they had planned everything in a careful bachelor way so as to produce a formal atmosphere. Christine later observed 'Walter made the mistake of asking us in.' The McWhinneys had not yet arrived, and, when they did, the atmosphere had changed from formal dinner to an informal party and grew more informal as the evening progressed. (Ernest was relieved to hear later that Walter had forgiven him and Christine 'for having rained on his parade'.) When, on their return home late that night, they approached the Rosedale bridge, which was close to our house, Zephyr, sensing home territory, pulled purposively on his lead. 'Thank God,' Ernest said, 'we have a seeing-eye dog with us.'

The second incident provided a memorable finale to Ernest's stay. On 5 October there was an installation ceremony for

Douglas LePan who had been appointed principal of University College, at University of Toronto. Following the ceremony, we had a reception at the president's house for academic colleagues and for special guests, the latter including the former governor general Vincent Massey. Ernest attended both the installation and reception. This was the first formal academic gathering he had been at since coming to Toronto, and I was concerned that he might find it heavy going and slip away to his room. I looked around anxiously and was most relieved to see that he was sitting on a sofa beside Vincent Massey, and that the two were having an animated conversation. When the party ended, I said to Ernest: 'You were having a good time with Mr Massey. What were you talking about?' 'Oh, we were talking about the superior character of the Maritimers, especially of the Nova Scotian. Mr Massey agreed with me so warmly that I almost tapped him on the shoulder and said "I am certain, Mr Massey, that you will go far." '

There was no doubt that Ernest greatly enjoyed his month in Toronto. But he wrote about it as if it were a fairy-tale, a Cinderella story that could never be repeated. For his work (and his peace of mind), he needed isolation and a particular place. Occasional associations with the great world were pleasant, even stimulating, but too much would wear down individuality and encourage a glossy conformism. And the 'place' for him was the house in Centrelea. It may have been imperfectly modernized – the electrical system was erratic, water was rarely hot or in sufficient quantities, and even the conversion of the furnace from wood to oil had brought more problems than satisfactions – but these practical matters never really worried Ernest, the most impractical of men. He simply made them the subject for his comic fantasies. The house remained his great good place. It is 'the only place,' he wrote, 'where I can generate a single idea with moving parts.'[26] When he was finally forced by illness to leave it, he ceased to write.

Ernest rarely spoke of his past to us. He was much too concerned about immediate questions to talk about past ones, and much too eager to find out what we thought or knew to soliloquize about himself. Our probes did not reveal any great detail. He produced dates and places for his life between graduation from Dalhousie in 1929 and the publication of *The Mountain and the Valley* twenty-three years later. But only the reading of his early letters and writings could reveal the pulse and colour of his literary apprenticeship, certainly one of the most extraordinary in the history of Canadian literature.

CHAPTER TWO

Apprenticeship

When we first met Ernest in 1953 he was forty-five years old, an age when most writers are in mid career. Yet *The Mountain and the Valley* was a first novel, for which there were no antecedents in the author's work. Was it a sudden, miraculous creation, and would this one book constitute the whole of his literary career? At forty-five Buckler liked to say that he was a farmer who wrote rather than a writer who farmed. But this was a pose. The reality was quite different.

The West Dalhousie community into which Ernest Buckler was born on 19 July 1908 had many of the characteristics of a frontier society, even though it was only a few miles away from one of the earliest settlements in North America. Certainly in Ernest's childhood, before the First World War, it was a subsistence community, with occasional cash income, stored snugly at home and reserved for rare purchases – presents at Christmas, an extraordinary outing at a travelling fair, wallpaper for the parlour, a new dress for mother. Short distances were still formidable in horse-drawn vehicles along narrow dirt roads; Bridgetown, for instance, was ten miles away, Annapolis somewhat farther, and a trip to either was a major undertaking. Oxen were used for all the heavy work on the farm, and in their slow, steady, imperturbable movements they were at one with the tempo of the community.

In other respects, however, it was an old rather than a frontier community. Ernest's great-grandfather, John Buckler, was a

United Empire Loyalist who came to West Dalhousie towards the end of the eighteenth century. There were also traditions, some of them no doubt authentic, of more direct connections with 'the old country.' On one occasion when Ernest and I visited the West Dalhousie Church, we met an elderly man with an erect bearing and good, strong features, who greeted Ernest warmly, 'Why, Ern Buckler, I haven't seen you for years.' They had known each other in the old days in West Dalhousie. Ernest, as usual with those who were not his intimates, responded impassively, and then, when his old acquaintance had gone, said with a touch of community pride, 'You know, his family was descended from the Dalhousies' (George Ramsay, 9th Earl of Dalhousie, was lieutenant governor of Nova Scotia from 1819 to 1828). Ernest liked to speculate about his Irish connection, indicated by his second name, Redmond, and more significantly by his mother's maiden name, Swift. He would refer to the tradition that his mother's family included the great satirist, and speculate half seriously that this accounted for his sombre view of society.

Whether or not any of these ennobling associations in the West Dalhousie community had a basis in fact, it was certainly true that the community was aware of values and interests beyond the daily routine necessary for existence. It was a dim, instinctive awareness certainly not supported even by the existence of an occasional family library. 'Certain families would "have a book" in the same sense that they might "have a phonograph." '[1] Ernest recalls from his boyhood days, an occasional Alger, Henty, or Zane Grey, and individual volumes, each a special family treasure, that he remembers only by their titles: *Lady Scarsdale's Daughters, Ishmael, Self-Raised from the Depths*. But the community placed a great emphasis on early schooling, and particularly on the results of the provincial exams that preceded the rare entrance of a local student to the high school in Bridgetown. Ernest describes in *Ox Bells and Fireflies* the community excitement that attended the ritual of writing the exams, and even more, the reception of the results.

The week the C's [the candidates] went off to 'write' (in their brand-new corduroy reefers or clouds of organdie), they were the center of everyone's thoughts. And the week in August when they were due to 'hear', the whole community quaked with each approach of the mailman. Hands trembled so they could scarcely open the envelope and draw out the sheet inside.

If in no case was the 'top torn off' this sheet (the top scrolly part proclaiming it to be a PASS certificate), a jubilant shout went relaying from hayfield to hayfield and those 'licencees' as they were called, were brandished aloft in the post office doorway, until the aprons of congregating women filled the air like a swarming of butterflies.[2]

Ernest was the most extraordinary student that the community had ever seen, and his facility both with words and numbers was so dazzling to teachers, fellow students, and his seniors that he was hailed as a prodigy and a genius. His own family rejoiced in his accomplishments. What he writes about a bright young boy in one of his short stories might have been written about him: ' ... the quick, nervous way of my mind seemed to make me the special one of the family.'[3] Ernest's sisters recall how their father, a quiet man who rarely showed his emotions, broke down and wept tears of joy when he saw Ernest's provincial examination report – a dazzling, unbroken line of almost perfect marks, such as had never occurred before in West Dalhousie.

Ernest was the only boy in the family. He had three sisters, Mona, closest to him in years (at five years his junior) and in affections (she was the model for Anna in *The Mountain and the Valley*), Olive, five years his senior, and Nelly, ten years his senior. There is no doubt that he was given a special position in the family and surrounded by love and a zealous concern. But the family devotion never resulted in a sense of superiority for the young boy or in isolation from the community, or by reason of a negative response, not unknown in such cases, in alienation from the family. Indeed its effect was to bathe the community in an idyllic glow, and to give to family ties (even when wearisome) an inviolable sanctity.

One incident in his childhood was never forgotten, indeed, seemed to flood his whole life. The actual incident is described in the short story 'The Bars and the Bridge.'[4] Going unwillingly on a cold, drizzly night to get the cows for milking, the young boy stops to pat the old family horse. The horse becomes irritated as the boy, in a sulky mood, persists. The boy recalls what happens. 'I can still see the big black haunch erupting, and the hoof, like a sudden devouring jaw, smack in front of my right eye.' Fortunately the horse is not shod and the boy escapes almost certain death. The story becomes a tribute to his father, who leaps an intervening fence, without stopping to let down a single bar, then holds the 'coloform' while the boy lies on the dining-room table and the doctor stitches the wound. In *The Mountain and the Valley*, David suffers a similar but much more serious wound when he falls to the floor from a high beam in the barn. For the young boy of the short story, 'two scars have bracketed my right eye since I was ten. They have faded to tiny commas visible only in cold or pallor.' David's scar never left him. It 'sickled, like a smile-scar, from the corner of his mouth to his left temple. It never rose to actual pain, but it seeped through his whole head like the penetration of a night fog that crept up from the marshes.'[5] The accident and the aftermath becomes for David the prologue to his withdrawal into a private world of loneliness and febrile fantasy. And for Ernest Buckler the actual accident of his childhood merges in his mind with a persistent headache that began some ten years later and constantly resisted medical diagnosis. In the syntax of his life the tiny commas of the young boy's scar became periods, not commas.

At the age of twelve, after one year at Bridgetown High School, he completed all requirements for university entrance – an academic record that was, I suspect, unparalleled in the annals of Nova Scotia education. Because of his extreme youth, the question of university entrance did not immediately arise, and was, in any event, beyond the immediate comprehension of a family with no tradition of university attendance, and with slender financial resources. But the idea of university attendance was not brushed aside. It would be five years before Ernest could be admitted to university, and during this time the financial problem might be solved. In the meantime, he worked on the farm, substituted briefly for a teacher at West Dalhousie, and kept his academic work fresh in tutoring sessions with the local Anglican clergyman. But the financial problems looked grim and insoluble, despite the self-denying economies of the family. Then, three years later, the problem was suddenly and romantically solved. A relative who held a senior position in a fashionable resort-hotel arranged for Ernest, aged fifteen, and his sister Nelly to join the staff, and each summer for the next six years he worked there in a variety of jobs – bellboy, waiter, desk clerk.

The hotel was Kent House, in Greenwich, Connecticut. It was a hotel to which guests returned regularly each year; they constituted a society at a dizzy remove from West Dalhousie, a society of wealth and easy sophistication. Fifty years later Ernest recalled this extraordinary translation to an exotic world.

Nothing could have been more incongruous than this unfledged bird from the Nova Scotian hills set down amidst these millionaired cockatoos of Belle Haven. I worked at a hotel called Kent House. Called, I say, although it tried desperately to be as anonymous as God. Nothing as vulgar as a sign, or an office that looked liked an office, or a printed menu (I remember one time a new headwaiter peacock-tailed all the napkins inside the water glasses and the management was horrified almost to seizures), etc. Guests were sieved (it was as hard to get into as Eton) right down to everything but a Wasserman; but nevertheless there were some wonderfully interesting people aboard.[6]

Some of the guests lived in untroubled isolation from the world around them. In the middle thirties Ernest corresponded briefly with an elderly lady who had been a regular resident at Kent House. She wrote sadly about changes during the previous ten years: the death of many fellow guests, and the catastrophe of Roosevelt. 'And with Roosevelt so crazy about the wild spending of other people's money. It makes everyone afraid. Stories are now going about that the man is out of his mind – it is easily believed.'[7] But there were other residents of a more lively temperament. Ernest remembered the actress, Betty Bronson, and how, when he was serving as desk clerk, she once came up to him and, without saying a word, pointed to an item on her bill that she questioned with an elegantly accusatory finger. He remembered, too, Professor Brander Matthews, the Columbia oracle, who one day pleaded with the switchboard operator not to call him Professor Matthews 'because it made him feel like a piano player in a whorehouse,' and George Parr McCutcheon, the author of the enormously popular 'Graustark books' and of *Brewster's Millions*, all of which Ernest had devoured.

A wealthy New Yorker at Kent House took a fancy to the young Buckler, so small and innocent in appearance, but bristling with information and opinion on a great variety of subjects, and proposed that he should work in his office during the day and attend Columbia at nights. Ernest went so far as to brave the canyons of Wall Street 'in a rather macabre combination of plus fours and patent leather shoes.' But he was terrified of the city, grew increasingly nervous as he was shunted from one interview to another, and ended up by tumbling down a flight of stairs and fleeing, happily uninjured, in embarrassment and shame to the security of Kent House. He later thanked his patron, and said that he had decided to stay in Nova Scotia. The incident, which he later saw in a comic light, probably left a lasting and searing impression and helped to inspire the anonymous urban landscapes that occur in his writing and symbolize the ultimate waste land of the spirit.

Ernest entered Dalhousie University in 1925 and graduated in 1929. He interrupted his college course for the year 1927–8, and returned home. The headaches that were to be a lifetime torture had begun, and these together with the sudden exposure to city living and the demands of a systematic programme of study undermined his health. His major subject was initially mathematics, but he switched to philosophy in his final year. In all likelihood, he would have persisted with mathematics had it not entailed associated work in physics. He was hopelessly inept in the laboratory, and once observed that 'he must have ruined at least three-quarters of the equipment.' But his love of mathematics remained with him. 'It's the only clean thing in the world,' he once observed. His two greatest pleasures, he once declared, were chopping wood and solving quadratic equations. He was a brilliant student in both mathematics and philosophy. The registrar of the university, Murray MacNeill, who was also a professor of mathematics, wrote that 'he is one of the outstanding students of the past decade.' The professor of philosophy, H.L. Stewart, wrote: 'He had a record of such distinction as I hardly ever remember in another student taking these classes since I came to Dalhousie in 1914. Mr. Buckler's combination of keen mental prowess with tireless industry and enthusiastic interest in his work were such as a teacher does not readily forget.'[8]

At Dalhousie he was known as the dedicated student. In the Dalhousie Year Book for 1929, he looks out in unsmiling seriousness, and the accompanying prose vignette gives a reinforcing impression. 'Ernest is first and foremost a brilliant student. Quiet and unassuming, he possesses a pleasing personality and lacks neither male nor female admirers. He has taken numerous classes in Philosophy and H.E. Taylor had better guard well his laurels.'

In later years Ernest never reminisced nostalgically about his Dalhousie days and never made any attempt to go to class reunions. But an undergraduate impression of the university belies his later indifference. 'I love old Dal. There's stability in the stone and mortar. Its old walls never shout greeting but there's always the stern but rugged and true welcome. They are like an undemonstrative father who waits forever and remembers you eternally ... return always moves one to tears almost.'[9]

Few friendships were made in the Dalhousie days. Hugh MacLennan was a contemporary (he graduated one year before Ernest), and in such a small community they could not avoid at least a passing acquaintance. But MacLennan was a big man on the campus – a champion tennis player and a scholar who was preordained to become a Rhodes scholar, and Ernest lived and worked in diligent obscurity. Another fellow student of campus fame was Ernest Howse, who was to be a moderator of the United Church and a preacher of power and erudition. In later life they exchanged books, and letters in which they reminisced about the secret passion each had for a popular co-ed.

What about the future writer? The only record of writing beyond classroom essays was a short piece for the *Dalhousie Gazette* on compulsory physical training. The hard fact is that Ernest not only didn't have a record of literary juvenilia, but read little outside the formal prescriptions of the curriculum, which included one obligatory English class. 'Dickens,' he wrote, 'bored me to yawns. Thackeray to tears.'[10] The only major writer he read at this time was Thomas Hardy, and his delight in Hardy, which continued into later life, carried him eagerly through all the novels. In a letter to a later correspondent, he analysed the nature of his love for Hardy. 'I know of no other place where one gets such intolerably moving pictures of the exquisite melancholy at the heart of things.'[11]

Buckler won an open fellowship in philosophy at the University of Toronto. He spent one year there, 1929–30, and at the end received his MA. The MA did not require a thesis, but the essay work was demanding. His papers contain two lengthy essays, 'Aristotle's Psychology of Conduct' and 'Prichard's Criticism of Kant's Theory of Knowledge.' The latter, the most impressive of the essays, is a systematic analysis of specific critical points raised by Prichard, with the great philosopher emerging undiminished. In one essay, 'Greek and Christian Views of the State,' a lively individual breaks through the serious young philosopher, although he still wears a Kantian cloak. He writes:

If Christianity may be said to have an economic policy explicit or implicit it might be socialism. The Christian problem regarding riches disappears. The difficulty is not that man is 'rich' but that man is 'richer than.' There is no objection to the goods of the world if they are shared. There is plenty for all and instead of man being rich, in socialism all will be equally poor and the needle's eye will have stretched and the camel shrunk so that a passage is possible. Socialism may seem contrary to the apparent extreme individualism of Christianity but the kingdom of God on earth is really what Kant calls a Kingdom of ends wherein the highest individuality is reconciled with social interdependence and where service is more or less perfect freedom.

Buckler never returned in any systematic way to the reading and study of philosophy. His philosophical year was a subject for light badinage. One of his fellow students studying in London, England, began his letter to him 'by asking me if Kantian categories were more like waffle-irons or jelly-moulds.'[12] To a friend who talked about his writing a philosophical novel, he replied tartly that philosophy, as in Kant, was an examination of how metaphysics is possible, and had nothing to do with imaginative writing. He was contemptuous of 'philosophical' articles in popular magazines. He complained about this occasional tendency even in his favourite magazine of the thirties, *Esquire*:

Every so often your more serious writers have a go at Philosophy. They are worse than Durant. Well maybe not quite that bad, you'd know I couldn't mean that bad, but someone should tell them that cosmic formulae are too complex, much too complex for them; and that you can't make a neat little story out of a Theory of Being, any more than you could make a ballet out of the Differential Calculus.[13]

Although his formal work at the University of Toronto left little impress, the year was in many ways a liberating one. 'My days at Dal.,' he wrote in his journal on 22 February 1936, 'were not the happiest of my life. My days at Trinity barring the health feature were. I learned not much philosophy but a good deal of the secret of good living.' The reference is to Trinity College in the University of Toronto where he was a member of the residence, an old apartment building just off the campus. The dean was the Reverend George Frederick Kingston, later archbishop of Nova Scotia and primate of all Canada, and Buckler admired him greatly. 'He lacks entirely that excruciating camaraderie which is often the subtlest form of condescension.'[14] And George Sidney Brett, his principal tutor in philosophy, was another inspiring figure. 'I was continually in awe of his giant intellect, literally convinced that he knew everything – but with his pure and distillate certainties (combined with a gentle charm of person), he set my thinking straight in more ways than I can count.'[15]

Buckler spent six more years in Toronto. We know comparatively little about those years. Most of what we do know comes from comments he made in later years. In those pre-computer days his mathematical abilities gave him an entrance to actuarial work and he spent all of his six years as he put it 'in the actuarial wing for anarchic dissidents at the Manufacturer's Life penitentiary.' A fellow dissident and Maritimer was Andrew Hill Clark, also a graduate student and a close friend, who eventually became head of the Department of Geography at the University of Wisconsin. (Forty years later he was appointed to the Claude Bissell professorship in Canadian-American relations at the University of Toronto, a visiting chair for one year, but he died before he could take up the appointment.) During this period Ernest moved into digs on Classic Avenue near the university, but still retained his association with the university and with graduate students he knew. He lived an innocuously bohemian life, bohemian by the standards of a city that still retained its Methodist aura. He recalls, for instance, in the journal he began on his return to West Dalhousie, an evening party,

at which the girl he was with put on her play suit and took two wilty cornflowers in her hot little hand and danced like Pavlova. The resonance and her dainty tread on the apartment floor must have carried some suggestion to the people below of Judgment. Whit was there, I recall – poor, good, bald-headed Whit. And the amazing young woman who could cross her eyes at will – a lifelong but unrealized ambition of my own.[16]

Another recollection evokes Toronto night-life in the thirties, and his description is reminiscent of the tone of an early Morley Callaghan novel. The recollection was prompted by the gift of a recording of *Porgy and Bess*.

Once, many years ago, I saw the play in a long-defunct Toronto theatre. I'll never forget the gripping moments in it. After Porgy, they played 'In Abraham's Bosom' – a much lesser play. Then, the original company broke up and started a sort of cabaret somewhere near the corner of Bloor and Yonge. You can imagine how long, in the Toronto of those days, blacks would be allowed to flourish there, and they were kicked out. My most vivid recollection is that one night I went there with a girl who got pretty smashed and insisted on sitting on the stairs outside and humming 'It Ain't Necessarily So.' Nothing could budge her and the fuzz was hovering near for some excuse to close the place. Meanwhile, I had somehow or other locked myself into the john! And so the whole staff, armed with knives and forks and other utensils tried to extricate me.[17]

On occasion he extended his social milieu beyond Toronto to Montreal. 'Grand City Montreal!' he wrote, 'the people there lack the absurd stuffiness of Torontonians and the rather clumsy wholesomeness of the Bluenose.'[18]

The bohemian life and its accompaniments were not at the heart of the Toronto years. Buckler had now decided that he would be a writer, and he set out to prepare himself for his self-determined course.

What brought about this crucial decision? If he accepted another fellowship now offered to him to study for his PHD, at the end lay at best an academic appointment, and he was, and remained throughout his life, neurotically resistant to speaking before an audience. Moreover, philosophy had lost its appeal. As he later observed, 'Kant and Leibnitz suddenly turned to meal and ashes in my mouth.' What reawakened his literary interests, dormant during his university days, was seeing good plays by first-class actors at Toronto's only commercial theatre in the thirties, the Royal Alexandra. You could get a seat in the second balcony for fifty cents, from which you looked down like a god on the stage far below, which yet seemed amazingly close and intimate. There is a letter in his papers, presumably never sent, written by the passionate playgoer. It is addressed to Katherine Cornell, whom he had just seen in a production of *Romeo and Juliet*. It begins, 'Your Juliet – every remembered silhouette exquisitely graceful your performance was electric with the fascination of a beautiful thing.' (As a young undergraduate, also in the second balcony, I would have agreed with this appraisal of Katherine Cornell's performance, which could be extended to all the principal actors, Basil Rathbone, Brian Aherne, Edith Evans, and an unknown actor, Orson Welles, playing Tybalt.) Buckler then informed Katherine Cornell that he was going to be a journalist and, if she would phone or write to wish him good luck, 'I should simply bounce with delight and gratitude.'

Another theatre great in young Buckler's eyes was Noel Coward. Many years later when he sold his papers to the University of Toronto Library, Buckler lamented the fact that now his 'callow and totally mistaken enthusiasms' would be revealed. 'When my generation were all young buds and thirsting for "sophistication" we thought that Noel Coward epitomized it. I even wrote him a fan letter, congratulating him on, of all things, an obvious heterosexuality (little did I know then!) which had struck "great blows toward the divorcement of footlights and fairies." '[19]

Buckler retained his interest in drama and the theatre throughout his life, and could always rely on a dramatic piece to bring in a restorative dollar from the CBC. But he early turned to what was to be his principal métier – prose fiction. During this period he filled the conspicuous gap in his university education, and read voraciously in modern fiction.

He wrote two stories for *The Trinity University Review*, one a rather laboured parody of the North American Indian romance. The other, 'No Second Cup,' was a solemn undramatic treatment of what was to be a central Buckler concern – the shifting loyalties of the country boy between the city and home. In the city the hero comes 'to look like those other grim ghosts

of the pavement, with their cramped eyes and febrile somnam-
bulism,' but, when he returns home, 'he could not tell his
mother that he had not come home – that he could not remember the bare, shrunken pastures – that everything old was
new and small.'[20] In 1936 Buckler did go home, but, after some
initial hesitations, he finally drank 'the second cup' and found
it sustaining.

Ostensibly Buckler returned to West Dalhousie because of
the breakdown in his health. His job in Toronto remained open
to him, and the plan was to return as soon as his health improved. In the meantime, he considered other jobs, and was
about to accept a teaching position in a school in Halifax when
his family, concerned about his health, argued against it. He
acquiesced in the family decision with some mild protests. 'The
absorption of my family in my affairs, although almost disastrously possessive at times, is nevertheless genuine and the
very core of its life. Every tentacle of its inner life is somehow
sensitive to my welfare and any devotion like that is a debt.'[21]
What he was saying, perhaps unconsciously but firmly, was
that his family believed in his genius and would give him the
time and the means to develop it as he saw fit.

His confidence in himself as a writer, although there was as
yet little evidence of it, is borne out by an impression given of
him by his friend, Andrew Clark, who came to see Ernest at
Centrelea thirty-five years later. 'It was a tremendous experience to have that long evening of talk with you – 35 years have
changed each of us so very little. You were then as you are
now, one of the world's free spirits with confidence (I used to
think of it with wonder as a kind of arrogance, too) that the
world would, somehow, provide a living for you. You had the
almost instinctive confidence of talent. As with myself, you
had another kind of talent to sustain you but when that required
persistence in a monotony of disenchantment you fled.'[22]

Clark's use of the word 'arrogance' is a subtle insight about
a man who outwardly was mild and self-deprecating. For Buckler had an iron self-assurance about his abilities. He had been
a phenomenally bright young boy, a brilliant student at uni-

versity, a scholar who could easily have established himself in the academic world. And now he was convinced that it was as a writer that he could most fully express his undeniable talents.

At first the writer worked secretly through a journal that he kept from November 1935 to March 1937. Like all journals kept by sensitive young men, Buckler's was often bitter in tone. He had not yet reconciled himself to his old home and the community in which he had grown up. He retained a good deal of the manners of the omniscient graduate student and of the urban sophisticate. In his journal he records an evening walk during which he was moved to talk to himself, 'the only audience that appreciates my inimitable wit.'

Recited to myself all my pet aversions, beginning with a travesty of the clergy, that lichen on the face of civilization. Next to rats, ministers are, in my opinion, the lowest form of life. That, mind you, is no criticism of Christianity; for praise a minister and you blaspheme against the Holy Ghost, they being diametrically opposed. I loathe ministers. Clammy with unction, sniveling with meekness and stinking to high heaven of hypocrisy, they get under my skin. One should disinfect after them, as one would after malaria mosquitos.

Buckler then went on to expose the errors of sentiment in the popular conception of the country man

whistling about his chores with nothing in his innocent little heart but God and his mavourneen. Nothing is falser. I find that most country people are intolerant to the point of persecution, festering inside with old hatreds, discontented with their lot and jealous of all and sundry who share the doubtful delights of the pavements. Try to convince one of them of something. I have never seen such invulnerability to the persuasions of syllogism.[23]

Later he reported gloomily on his attendance at a school Christmas concert, an event that in *The Mountain and the Valley* he sees, with wonder and solemnity, through the eyes of his hero. Now the concert has lost all its enchantment. Per-

haps the years, with their increasing burden of false sophistication, have actually brought a decline, perhaps the country
Christmas concert never was more than a crude charade, and
Buckler, the cool observer and seasoned playgoer, sees it in its
true light.

Last night, went with rather high expectations of amusement, to the
local school concert – in the same lamp-lit, ramshackle, mice-holed
structure that saw the nativity of my own education. The whole thing
was rather awful. I find that I have no sentiment for my own early
beginnings; and the performance wasn't bad enough to be funny.
Recitation after repetitious recitation until always nervous when I do
not share the appreciation the rest of the audience feels, my face
twitched constantly with a false smile. Looking about at the husky,
addled youth that was represented I thought how doubtful a blessing
was the discomfort of intelligence – particularly intelligence without
health. Not one face of a boy my age showed the slightest trace of
thought or strain.[24]

What outlet beyond his journal could Buckler find for this
vein of caustic comment? He had recently immersed himself
in American magazines of a literary and satiric bent, and he
had been attracted to the writing of Alexander Woollcott, who
was one of the presiding masters of the school of light raillery.
Perhaps Woollcott would recognize a kindred voice and give
him advice. He wrote a letter to the great man, which began
in this way: 'This is not a fan letter – with your great volume,
its acreage would be pathetically inadequate. What bothers me
is this. I write as well as you do, but get paid much less.'[25]
Woollcott fortunately never saw the letter. Buckler had included a few examples of his own writing, and Woollcott's
secretary wrote that her chief never read manuscripts. Buckler
now adopted a more indirect and personal technique. He sent
his letter to the correspondence section of *Esquire*, which was
entitled 'The Sound and the Fury.' Without knowing it he was
writing directly to the editor, Arnold Gingrich, who took a
personal interest in correspondents, especially those who com-

mented on his precious magazine. Gingrich was a literary generalist who quickly enlisted talent, whether recognized or emerging. He was *Esquire*'s creator and its presiding spirit. He had completely transformed a trade paper about men's fashions, retaining the hearty male emphasis, with a bow to bawdry, and titillating drawings. The signature here was the regular cartoons of current beauties – invariably long-legged and scantily attired. After their creator, they were known as the Petty girls. They have, said Buckler, 'a sort of waxen perfection like false teeth.'

But at the same time Gingrich made *Esquire* a leading literary magazine of the thirties. The list of contributors reads like a check-list of the most important American writers of the times: George Jean Nathan, H.L. Mencken, Theodore Dreiser, Scott Fitzgerald, Ernest Hemingway ('The Snows of Kilimanjaro' first appeared in *Esquire*), Sinclair Lewis, Ezra Pound, E.E. Cummings, Tennessee Williams, John O'Hara, Dorothy Parker, John Dos Passos, Peter DeVries, and one Canadian, Morley Callaghan. When Buckler wrote his first letter to 'The Sound and the Fury' in March 1937, most of these authors had already appeared in its pages. This letter, like the others that followed (the highest concentration, five, coming during 1937) grew out of what Buckler called 'a passion to annotate.' He brashly assumed a position of authority, like a bright graduate student holding forth to his fellows, or like a court jester with a licence to criticize and ridicule the high and mighty. In his first letter he suggests that George Jean Nathan's 'bayoneted sarcasms would be more to the point if he himself had ever shown any conspicuous talent for the writing of good, or even successful plays.' In a later letter (November 1937), he reports that he has read Nathan's play *The Avon Flows*, and comments, 'All I can say is, Mr. Nathan can't write Shakespeare like Bacon did.' He complains that the articles by Havelock Ellis and Dr Adler for *Esquire* 'lack entirely the unsugared candour which characterizes their scientific brochures less dependent on editorial subsidy.'[26] He begins an unremittingly scathing attack on Scott Fitzgerald: 'Any of his work published in the last ten years has been, as far as his early alleged genius is concerned, quite posthumous.'[27]

Buckler's tough critical attitude sustained through all his letters did not indicate his displeasure with *Esquire*. Indeed, he thought highly of it and warned the editor that he should not consider too many changes in the editorial policy he had established: a ballast of short stories; articles of a general nature, often about European issues; a number of special departments dealing with books, movies, the theatre, music, records, broadcasting.

Now that you have outgrown your original self-consciousness about Rabelais' mantle, and a certain forced boisterousness which located in Chicago, may have been due not to heredity but to environment, and which suggested a bookkeeper (he of that profession next to the oldest the most maligned) on a spree, the product you have finally arrived at is almost entirely satisfactory.[28]

Gingrich thought highly of Buckler's contributions to 'The Sound and the Fury.' From the very beginning he responded happily to Buckler's combination of seriousness and flippancy. When Buckler concluded his first letter with the request that it should not be labelled 'with some glib inadequacy like "thinks Dos Passos obscure," ' the published heading read "Thinks Dos Passos Opaque." The second letter was headed 'Encore,' the third 'In and about E.B.,' the fourth 'The one Man S & F,' the fifth, 'Buckler, like the Brook,' the sixth 'Buckler's Bit,' the seventh 'our Shield and our Buckler.' Finally in the eighth (January 1939), Buckler emerged from 'The Sound and the Fury' and was given an editorial salute. Gingrich wrote: 'Our favourite author is a guy named Ernest Redmond Buckler, who lives in Bridgetown, Nova Scotia. This is no sudden crush – he's been our favourite author for years now.' In his book about the early days of *Esquire*, Gingrich recalled that his high estimate of Buckler was shared by many other readers of *Esquire*.

People began writing in that they'd prefer to save their issues and read them only after Buckler's exegetical comments on them had appeared in subsequent numbers; some other people wrote that they'd rather read what Buckler said about the issues than read the magazines themselves. And some began saying they hoped I was paying Buckler a lot of money, because he was worth Hemingway, Fitzgerald, Dos Passos, Dreiser, and all the rest put together.[29]

Other readers agreed with Gingrich. A young man named Ted Bentley, living in Hollywood and aspiring to write lyrics for popular songs, began a correspondence with Buckler that lasted until the late seventies. (He and Buckler never met. Bentley redirected his creative talents to public relations, in which he prospered.) After reading Buckler's first three letters in 'The Sound and the Fury,' he wrote: 'Every once in a blue moon ... I stumble across a prose writer with a style so incisive, so flippantly delightful, that it disturbs me. I found that style in Heinrich Heine, in Oscar Wilde, in James Huneker – I find it in you. What is said is not important ... Like Wilde, you say most anything in order to say it clearly.'[30]

At least two of Buckler's enthusiastic readers were professional writers of note. Manuel Komroff was a prolific writer and editor whose short stories appeared regularly in *Esquire*. Like Bentley, he was impelled to write to Buckler about his contributions to 'The Sound and the Fury.' 'You are certainly *Esquire*'s star performer, and I think you should write your letters a shade longer and submit them as critical articles. That is evidently your style and it is most devastating. The ten-pins fall in all directions and great names mean nothing. It is lively and most unique. It hits with explosive force. The big ones are not bled white, they just turn white and stay that way.'[31] As with Bentley, this launched a correspondence that continued until Komroff's death in 1974. As with Bentley too, he and Buckler never met. An even more dramatic endorsement came from Burton Rascoe, *Esquire*'s book critic and an editorial consultant to Doubleday Doran. He sent Buckler a telegram: 'Your letter in March *Esquire* is superb and shows an excellent sense and command of vigorous, effective English prose. As literary advisor to a publishing house I am anxious to see what you consider your best unpublished work.'

All this was heady stuff to a writer, still uncertain of his calling, and making his first entry into the literary world. He had chosen to make his début as critic and wit, a role usually reserved for assured maturity, and he had been accepted immediately as an accomplished performer. Was it absurd for the farmer from an obscure hamlet in a remote part of North America to think of himself as an authoritative critic and pundit? A great inner self-confidence always triumphed over Buckler's bouts of self-belittlement and despair. He would accept the role and build his career upon it. A series of letters to various magazines and newspapers followed, in each of which he put forward his name for a regular feature. He wrote to *Judge* offering himself as drama critic in succession to George Jean Nathan. He wrote to the *New Yorker* that 'quite seriously, I think the spirit of my stuff (giving it a very special praise of my own) matches very closely that of the *New Yorker*.'[32] And to his great mentor, the editor of *Esquire*, he wrote:

... if you've been looking for someone to fill that vacant spot in *Esquire* with book reviews as honest as Hemingway, as keen as frost, as arresting as red on black, and as much more lively and readable than the books themselves, as biographers are than lives, here am I, then, take me. God knows I've been under a bushel long enough.[33]

The letters to 'The Sound and the Fury' were the phenomenal outcome of a happy merging of several things: Buckler's delight in language, fed by years of formal study and private reading, his youthful confidence in the soundness of his judgments, and a talent for invective gleefully displayed. Together they created a 'persona' that was exactly suited to *Esquire* and gave him a sudden eminence he could not sustain. The samples of 'other writing' – early stories, humorous pieces, a critical piece on Noel Coward – that he sent to Gingrich and Rascoe were disappointing, and each told him so in no uncertain tones. Gingrich wrote that 'the efforts at feature writing seemed stiff and terribly self-conscious, as if he were aware for the first time of speaking "prose," like a boy standing up to recite something in school.'[34] Buckler recalled Gingrich's response to a long article which he himself described as 'turgid with undigested metaphysics and cataracted with opacity.' 'Good God,' said Gingrich, 'I thought Duns Scotus had died long ago.' Rascoe was even more devastating:

I had the impression from your letter in *Esquire* that you had some unpublished book length manuscripts, perhaps a novel. What you have sent me are 'exercises' rather than evidences of sustained endeavor. You won't mind my saying (for I believe you have definite talent and will be heard from in time) that I think that, except for the first sentence which is unusually good, your notes on Noel Coward are definitely bad, and that I can see no merit in the synopsis of the 'Odyssey of a Five Dollar Bill.'

Knuckle down, please, work like the devil, write and write and write some more. You have a nice sense of words and the style you employed (perhaps unconsciously) in the Esquire letter is lively and distinctive.[35]

Buckler took these criticisms to heart. For the time being he abandoned his role as critic, wit, and rhetorician. He made only two more contributions of a related kind. One was a prize-winning letter in a contest to describe the special qualities of *Coronet*, a new magazine launched by Gingrich, conceived of as a small artistic jewel both in format and content. Buckler harnessed his rhetoric to unbuttoned praise. '*Coronet* is at once a mine of information, a feather to humour, an introduction to wonder, a passport to beauty and a theatre for the incalculable transfiguration of art.' For this (and a good deal more of the same) he received one hundred dollars, the first money he had earned by his pen. The second contribution was a series of radio dramas conceived of as comedies of the sexes in which estranged couples spoke to each other in brittle Cowardese. In 1941 three of these were accepted by the CBC and they constituted Buckler's unheralded Canadian début.

Gingrich, like Rascoe, had urged Buckler to try his hand at fiction, and Buckler realized that this had been his real goal ever since he had left Toronto and had decided to be a writer. His journal, as we have seen, was an outlet for his frustration and a release for his satiric wit, and this vein he had worked with great success in the letters to *Esquire*. But underneath the flippancy, and occasional savagery, of the journal was a self-imposed apprenticeship for the future novelist. He had no illusions about the difficulties of shifting from elaborate expository prose to fiction:

Fiction, the easiest thing to read, is the hardest thing, I find, to write. In my case, where ill health has held me back from any experience more vivid than an evening with embroidery floss, it is very difficult to spin like the spider, from within myself, any web of convincing lies. So often one packs one's kit and absents oneself in hidden places to write only to find that one has forgotten to bring along something to write about. Another thing, I wait too long on inspiration. There's a recipe for inspiration like every other wine. Press the grapes of experience and let them ferment. Then, when the lid blows off, get out the typewriter. Writing is a great deal more a matter of labor than of luck. If you're a sissy and like to become paunchy and, like the voluptuous Romans, from easy living, the spade is more your tool than the pen.[36]

The journal contains no examples of extended fictional exercises. He is content with set-piece descriptions, mood pieces that are elaborate and awkward versions of the brilliant precision of similar passages in the novels. A moonlight night inspires these ruminations.

The air was crisp and clear and shafts of the moonlight, luminous, slightly pink, cut through it like broad ribbon of slow lightning. The moon itself, quiet and unhurried, hung still in the sky, aloof but near, so near that it seemed that one might touch it with a long willow pole. The snow lay with the solemnity of a bride's white shroud, coloured at last after its dizzied flights through the air. Once into the woods, patient and no longer clumsy, relaxed with the hypnotism of the moon, the immaculate beauty of the scene was like a sweet shock. Here, the path was not bright with the first glitter of the outside world but jagged fingers of the thin glow lay stretched here and there across it with a little ghostliness. Only in the small clearings were the thick shadows again completely conquered; and even here the fingers of the woods quietly menaced with its greedy tongues of opacity that, themselves rooted, the trees sent out to guard their secrecy.[37]

He records 'a harvest of ideas ... each some little Leibnitzian facet of human existence ... Later, some time, when my novel is under way, I will skim off the risen cream.' Here is a collection of such facets: a curious menage of Noel Coward, Bergson, *Esquire* bawdry, and an anticipation of themes that will be developed in short stories and novels.

... the tastelessness of revenge ... encompassed with trivialities ... if she could somehow harness the voluptuousness inadequately managed by her taut brassiere ... seeking simplicity and peace, one does not recognize the track of dullness ... floating about willy-nilly in a taxi-cab ... barbs of ambition impinging on my peace of mind ... it is impossible to be really nasty in a boiled shirt ... to skewer him neatly on an adjective, he might have been by Lord Chesterfield out of Emily Post ... short story idea: the winter dusk when there was a grim silent clash of feelings in the house and I, a small, bewildered child took my sled and went coasting but couldn't quite forget something vague that kept troubling me ... their naked, undefended faces were curiously embarrassing ... the mute threnody of a bruised heart ... he was patronizing, even to sunsets ... poverty and capitalism are contemporary but unrelated ... moth-eaten dignity ... flatulent with suspicion ... searching tendrils of pain ... redundant as young love ... his supercilious gaze roaming about the room had the effect of slapping each one, individually, in the face ... X's cleverness is obscurely irritating. Encountering the same thing in a face ... the first impulse is to slap it ... the trouble with writing plays against war, the people who make wars don't go to plays ... quiet lagoons of thought ... I am

too busy to clutter up my time with civilities ... well up among the
immortals ... the log that crushed his chest had a stupid pointed snout.
Curious that inanimate things have, in their heaviness, the power of
death to the living ... in the tense caution of country hospitality, one
feels as if an arsenal of eyes were focused, critically and pitilessly, on
one's minutest facial grimace ... [38]

The same double movement apparent in the journal takes place
in 'The Sound and the Fury' letters: beneath the caustic rhetoric
of the critic is the anxious searching of the artist. In all the
letters, he had given some attention to the short stories, and
in a passage written after his rebuff from Rascoe, he described
the agonies of the writer of fiction and the ideal qualities he is
trying to embody in his own writing:

The best fiction in *Esquire* may appear childishly simple and easy
but that's just why it's good. Try to duplicate it yourself, you who
'can't but teach.' You'll find it's like sleight of hand. You watch ever
so carefully but you can't see the trick and even if you do, you find
your own hands too clumsy ever to duplicate it, with the same illusion ... Try it yourself. You'll find that what sounds fresh and compelling and strong inside your head looks trite and stringy and thin
on paper ... You try to improve it. You shift the furniture of your
sentences about, ceaselessly; your conscious and subconscious both
work on it, sleeping and waking. Till some night when you're tossing
in bed, you suddenly get an arrangement that strikes you as perfect.
And you're as excited and jumpy as a sophomore with his first box
of safes. So excited you can't sleep. But when you get up, tired, in
the morning, and write it down and read it over, you see it's still thin
and dead ... and you feel quiet – sick all that day. With the fear that
maybe you'll never be able to get into your words, like Manuel Komroff does, that subtle, intricate, simple something which crystallizes
their impact like a string precipitating a saturated solution ... that
you'll never learn the eerie magic of John Steinbeck, with his strange
accumulative hypnosis ... that you'll never be able to put on paper
the very feel and smell of the sweet clean earth, like Jesse Stuart ...

Then you'll be saddened and lenient and have a little more sympathy, perhaps, with artists who, even as you, are beset with that same maddening sense of disparity between conception and performance.[39]

Previously Buckler had sung the praises of Hemingway, who occupied, in his critical hierarchy, a place far above the writers he mentions in this passage. (Jesse Stuart was a popular writer of the day, a prolific contributor to *Esquire*, usually of stories about rural life in Virginia, written with the simplicity and directness of the folk tale.) Hemingway, he wrote, was 'utterly simple like the really great. There is not in his entire work a single complexity or effect that is synthetic.'[40] His harsh attitude towards Scott Fitzgerald, another *Esquire* great, clarifies his own position. He thought that Fitzgerald's style 'seems to get in the way of his thought,' and that his reliance on a specific social and moral milieu tipped his fiction over into journalism.

When Buckler wrote of the agonies of the writer of fiction, he could now draw from his own experience. When the journal came to an end, he began a novel, which he modestly called 'Excerpts from Life.' The hero is called Eric Redmond, but at an early stage Eric slips into David, and we are clearly moving in the direction of *The Mountain and the Valley*. 'Excerpts from Life' begins with a Hardyesque incident: Martha Legros, an easy-going, sensual woman is stung by her husband's unjustified accusations of infidelity. She leaves home in a distracted state and is found later drowned in 'the baptizing pool' of the local brook. This incident hovers in the background of Buckler's first published story, 'One Quiet Afternoon' (*Esquire*, July 1940). The young boy of the story, who is taunted by his fellows for his tenderness towards Martha, watches her as she runs crying towards the baptizing pool. A few minutes later, the boy sees a strange car passing through the village and catches a glimpse of 'a cool-looking woman.' He thinks, 'there is the kind of woman I will marry,' and promptly forgets Martha.

'One Quiet Afternoon' was an attempt to write an *Esquire* story, which Buckler had skittishly described in his first letter to 'The Sound and the Fury.' 'They present to the layman no deciphered plot; and would lend themselves beautifully to those curiously insipid headings with which you obscure their titles already enigmatic to the point of Gertrude Stein.'[41] In a more serious vein, Buckler would have said that the *Esquire* story at its best was a meditation on the contrast between appearance and reality, between the outer and the inner, and that in his story he had tried to realize *Esquire*'s ideal. His best stories would follow in the same vein, with an increasing concession to linking the meditation to action.

'One Quiet Afternoon' was the launching of Buckler's career as a serious writer. (The *Coronet* piece could be looked upon as simply a prescribed exercise.) Presumably Buckler received the usual *Esquire* fee of $250, and this in itself was a notable event. But the dazzling significance was that he had been accepted as a writer of fiction not unfit to join a group of the undeniably great, and, henceforth, no editorial rejection would dent his self-confidence. His jubilation overflows the letter he wrote to Gingrich on receiving the letter of acceptance.

I'm trying hard not to let myself go and tell you that, by God, you're the damndest swellest decentest guy alive. Me here, a bird with no pull whatever ... my name means nothing to nobody ... and you a guy at the top, where all the other guys forget the bottom. And still, with nothing to gain, you encourage me and help me until finally I land a story smack into the fairest, squarest, truest, finest, goddam magazine going! I'm trying not to let myself go like that. But you gotta know something of what the acceptance of my first story has meant to me ... how it feels to know I have done the one thing which undone would have made death intolerable ... what it has meant to my people, my own blood-people here in the country ... the sweet satisfaction in telling the friends who have kept far more loyal faith in me than I ever had in myself that their faith has not been entirely unjustified ... I wish I could tell you something of all that, truly, without sounding phoney or suck-hole ... but isn't it hell, when a guy needs the best words he's got, they seem to hold out on him.

Well I can tell you one thing, anyway ... the check was a godsend. I wasn't as hard up for postage stamps as Jesse Stuart, but my typewriter was mortgaged to the hilt. And now the whole damn family can have things.

Perhaps when the excitement has died down I can write you something more coherent and restrained. But just now we're all shouting across the ploughed-land from one neighbour's house to another, every hook on the old party line is down, and my mother is standing with her apron on in the road, waving the letter wildly to Aunt Lizzie and crying like I was dead. Aunt Lizzie, God bless her, is running and crying, too. I can't help feeling a little sad, though, to think that the happiest moment of my life is almost past. By God, I believe there's a story there![42]

CHAPTER THREE

Promise Fulfilled

The Mountain and the Valley

By the time Buckler published his first novel, *The Mountain and the Valley*, in 1952, he had established himself as a professional writer. The process had begun with *Esquire*'s publication in 1940 of his first story, and gained momentum steadily during the ensuing decade. He wrote now from the security of his own house and farm at Centrelea (legally owned by his mother, who lived with him and supported him in a career that many of his neighbours must have thought of as an incomprehensible aberration). The farmer who wrote turned into the writer who chose to live on a farm.

Although the pressure to earn money in what was still, to a great extent, a subsistence economy was not great, Buckler longed for a steady income, if only to justify his errant profession. The steady income from his writings did not come until the seventies, and then only on a modest scale. In the sixties he wrote to an American editor that he lived 'from pen to mouth on the perpetual brink of insolvency.'[1] In a daily journal that he kept, briefly and laconically he recorded his slow rise in cash income from $800.00 in 1949 to $3,000.00 in 1953, the latter made up of royalties from *The Mountain and the Valley*, payments for short stories, and $189.77 from the sale of a few pigs and one cow.

In the forties he steadily pursued the idea of a column in a magazine, which, he thought, would assure him of a regular income. *Esquire* had not been impressed by his prose contributions (except for the letters) and other American magazines had not responded to the pretentious proposals of an unknown colonial. He turned to a Canadian magazine where he had received some initial encouragement – *Saturday Night*. The editor, B.K. Sandwell, although turning down some material that Buckler had sent to him as unsuitable for his magazine, welcomed the introduction 'to one who seems likely to be an important figure in Canadian literature.'² A second contribution a month later – a humorous sketch – elicited a more positive reply from Sandwell. 'It is so damned good that I simply can't make up my mind to pass it up. As a matter of fact, the one thing against it is that it is a little too damned good for S.N. – too literary. But there will be a fair percentage of readers who will get its flavor.'³ Sandwell returned later to his theme of the fatal superiority of Buckler's writing. 'It would be like putting a string quartet to perform in a band shell in the open air, with fireworks going on half a mile away – as they used to at the Toronto Exhibition.'⁴ Eventually, however, in 1947, *Saturday Night* decided to take a chance on Buckler as a columnist – 1500 words at 2 cents a word.

Buckler wrote regularly for *Saturday Night* for one year. He adopted a sober style, eschewing the extravagant wit of the *Esquire* letters. He covered a wide variety of stories – portraits of local celebrities, impressions of places, reflections on social and economic issues, the inadequate facilities in the Maritimes for treatment of the mentally ill, the tragic butchering of orchards, the nature of the Maritime appeal. He couldn't write dully on any subject, and, passionate Maritimer that he was, he instinctively recoiled at writing that was even a shadow of advertising prose. He thus reflected on the appeal of the Maritimes for intellectuals and artists like John Dewey and Jessica Tandy. 'They don't come all this way to see a picturesque rock or a limpid marsh. Maybe we are incredibly uniform. Maybe that's it, we got rhythm. Maybe we are incredibly untransmutative. Maybe that's it, we're "a rock in a weary land." '⁵

The *Saturday Night* column was a source of income but was not central to his literary ambitions: his job was to write fiction.

The forties were given over to the writing of short stories, and Buckler pursued publication with tenacity and on a wide front. He brushed aside rejections (which certainly equalled, if they did not exceed, acceptances) and persisted. He had some successes (financial rather than literary) with wide-circulation American magazines, notably *The Ladies Home Journal* and *Colliers*, but most of his stories appeared in Canadian magazines, *Atlantic Advocate, Chatelaine, Saturday Night*, and especially *Maclean's*.

Buckler was always nervous and apologetic about his short stories. When a volume of his selected short stories appeared in 1975, he wrote to me:

When the advance copies reached me, I couldn't read them for wincing. It seemed to me that they were not just plain ruddy bad (the stories), but (with the kind of nakedness of everything, that even my better writing rose to) *embarrassing* ... I do have a few excuses for even the molasses of sentimentality. At the time most of the stories were written, I had no idea that I was a 'writer,' or that they would even be preserved. And, at that time, it was impossible to market a story that didn't have an overall – to use a terrible word – 'upbeat' (Just as to-day you can't possibly sell a story that isn't made up of soot-picking, nullity and/or kinky fucking.) I suppose it was whoring on my part, to keep the market in mind, but when one is starving, one does strange things.[6]

These were harsh judgments, but the weight of critical opinion is against Buckler. Certainly, there were formula stories, especially variations on the theme of Christmas as the miraculous time of revelation and renewal. A series of stories appearing in *Maclean's* clearly belong in the Buckler canon. These were 'Penny in the Dust,' 'The Quarrel,' 'The Clumsy One,' and 'The Rebellion of Young David.' (They were all selected by Robert Chambers for his anthology, *The Rebellion of Young David and other stories*.) The first three anticipated characters and some of the main themes of *The Mountain and the Valley*. We have the father, outwardly stern and inarticulate, whose actions proclaim his integrity and reveal his deep emotions; the mother, who has a priestly devotion to her household tasks and a love for her husband that is intense and yet vulnerable; the elder brother, a clumsy child with words, a leader among men in the field and workshop; and, prominently, the younger brother who has a magical way with words and numbers, and a fumbling ineptness with things. The theme in all these stories is the deep and subtle tensions in the family and their eventual resolution, often with pain and misunderstanding. The fourth story, 'The Rebellion of Young David,' departs from the auto-biographical, and was incorporated as part of the background of a character in *The Cruelest Month*.

The general tone of the first three stories is retrospective. The narrator, who is close to the David of *The Mountain and the Valley*, remembers events that took place deep in the past. In the first two he reaches back into childhood: he recalls his grief at losing a shiny penny that his father had given him, and he relives the first time he went with his parents to the Exhibition at Annapolis Royal, a magic day in anticipation but clouded over by a smouldering quarrel between his father and mother. In 'The Clumsy One,' he is reliving an incident in his youth when he callously erected a wall between his college friends and the brother who knew only the words and ways of the farm.

These stories are all meditations on the inner life; the events are important only insofar as they illuminate that life. They begin with a preliminary generalization or question, and the story becomes an illustrative parable. In 'The Penny in the Dust' it is a question about the true nature of a father who seems to be 'an inarticulate man a little at sea with an imaginative child.' The first section of 'The Quarrel' poses a precise psychological question. 'Do you know what quarrelling is like between a man and a woman to whom the language of quarrelling is an alien tongue?' 'The Clumsy One' begins with a generalization about the relationship between brothers who love and yet torment each other. 'The Rebellion of Young David' begins with a reminder of the mystery of the child's inner life.

Buckler's success in placing his stories with *Maclean's* brought him the friendship and support of W.O. Mitchell, who had taken over as fiction editor in 1948. Buckler admired Mitchell as novelist and valued him as critic. When Mitchell characterized a Buckler story as a 'clinker,' 'too exotic and confused,' Buckler instantly saw the truth of the judgment. And when Mitchell praised a story, he knew that he had succeeded. In accepting 'A Penny in the Dust' for publication, Mitchell wrote: 'The characterization of the child and his father are sure: the story is quite moving without being mawkish or sentimental. I think you've done a lovely and sensitive job in showing the relationship between the child and father.'[7] Each statement struck Buckler as a wording of his own innermost thoughts. Buckler's story, 'The Quarrel,' also published in *Maclean's*, won the magazine's fiction contest in 1949, and Buckler knew that the decision had Mitchell's warm support. He wrote to his American agent, 'I continue almost daily to be grateful to that wonderful guy and expert writer, W.O. Mitchell, who keeps up a sort of unobtrusive press-agentry for me whenever he gets a chance.'[8]

Mitchell's 'press-agentry' no doubt aroused an increasing interest among Canadian publishers in the novel on which it was known Buckler was engaged. He had letters of inquiry from John Gray of Macmillan and from Sybil Hutchinson of McClelland and Stewart. But for his novel, by the late forties well on the way to completion, he had entrusted himself to his American agent, and hoped that he could make some impact on the huge American market, with a generous overflow in Canada through an associated Canadian publisher. Buckler had high hopes of an acceptance from the Atlantic Monthly Press. A short story for *The Atlantic Monthly* had been turned down, but had elicited a letter from the editor, Edward Weeks, who wrote that 'we feel as if you are an almost contributor, and we hope you will try again.'[9] Subsequently he was greatly heartened by news that the Atlantic Monthly Press had taken a first option on the novel. But the Atlantic reader, whose report echoes with what John Updike has called 'the too-comfortable cadences and jargon of the critical voice,' turned down the novel flatly, and the head of the press accepted his reader's judgment. The reader wrote: 'This man is an earnest hopeful who I suspect aspires to emulate Hardy but whose love for words and language blinds him to the importance of place and technique.'[10] Buckler wrote a lively letter defending his novel against the criticism. But he was depressed none the less. Would the labour of ten years or more come to nothing. As 1952 opened with no sign of acceptance, he sank into a mood of dark melancholy. On 5 January he wrote in his diary: 'No mail of any exciting kind for days. Nothing interesting ever happens. I can't get a line on any darned plot and time is slipping. Low and hopeless. Die Gottendamerung.'

Then suddenly the gods returned. Another major publisher, Henry Holt of New York, found the novel as good as the Atlantic had found it bad. The approval letter of acceptance on 10 January glowed with praise of the book and optimism about its reception. Holt was confident that it would be both a critical and financial success. Jonathan Loff, Holt's assistant editor, seemed in his letter of analysis to be writing a point by point rebuttal to the Atlantic's contumelious dismissal. 'Usually,' he wrote, 'a novel is known by one of three criteria: plot, character, or style. The M & V is among the few to fulfill all these standards. The plot is real and solid and substantial; the characters, all very much alive, are created with warmth and sensitivity and dimension, and the literary style knows a fluidity and vividness and vitality and accuracy that is a delight.'[11]

Thirteen years before, with the publication of his short story in *Esquire*, Buckler had invaded 'the creative field outside which,' as he said, 'I have lingered so long, like a hungry child gazing into a confectioner's window.'[12] Since then he had earned the right, by the publication of more short stories and journalistic articles, and by the performance of radio dramas, to be known as a professional. But to him the novel was the real test; a successful novel that was critically acclaimed could give him the right to pass the confectioner's shop and to join the table when authors foregathered. If *The Mountain and the Valley*, a novel that he said was 'very intensely felt,' found no publisher, then he would be left with the small consolation of minor literary journalism, to remain forever a farmer who occasionally wrote. The letter that he wrote to Arnold Gingrich on the acceptance by *Esquire* of his short story is the exultant cry of the young man who has won a coveted prize. The letter that he wrote to William Raney, executive editor of Henry Holt and Co., is the heart-felt celebration of the mature artist whose worth is now known.

I can't begin to tell you what a tremendous uplift your acceptance of my novel has given me. But ... and here I go, I guess, letting my hair down hell west and crooked, so you'll probably say, as we say in these parts, 'I felt foolish *for* him' ... but, anyway, if you'll think back to the first moment you knew that someone you loved loved you, and square it, and then add the one Christmas morning as a child which you'll always remember, and square that total, and then multiply by the feeling of the first drink warming in you when you're with a special friend you've just been able to tell good news to, and then add the feeling when someone has been desperately ill sometime and the doctor comes out of the room and says, 'It's going to be allright,' smiling, and then cube *that* ... it may give you a rough idea. Perhaps I should stop right there, or you'll think I'm trying to lay it on. But really I'm not. The day the news came I was sitting in my room, gazing out over the bleak indrawn winter fields, quite stopped in the writing problem I was trying to work out, and feeling that frightening loneliness you get when you think: Even if I *could* turn out something good, where's the listening – except for that awful almost-taunting listening of the objects in the room when you've struck an impasse like that. Then the news came, and suddenly the whole face of things shifted like the crowd's face at the station shifts when the one you've given up as not having come (you're just turning for home) all at once steps off the train.[13]

The best of the short stories of the forties obviously emerged from the imaginative vision that was fashioning *The Mountain and the Valley.* In a general sense, the novel extends and enriches the short stories. The novel, for instance, is also retrospective. It begins with a scene that will be completed only at the end of the novel. The hero, David, is thirty years old, the date (the precise date is not given) in the mid-forties. The setting is cheerless and austere – December before the snow, when colour has disappeared from the landscape and the light is pale and uncertain. Then, in the second chapter, the years surge backward: it is around 1920 (again the precise date is not given) and the young man of thirty is a child of five or six. It is April, stirring with the promise of warmth. 'The whole morning glistened fresh as the flesh of an alder sapling when the bark was first peeled from it to make a whistle.'[14] Then we move forward, by roughly five-year leaps, until we have reached the time and place of the first scene. The opening scene had already indicated the main characters of the novel, and glanced at distinguishing characteristics and foreshadowed a number of the principal events.

The novel, like the best short stories, is meditative; Buckler is concerned with the inner movements of the mind far more than he is with external events. His concern is with the tensions that arise between people, often between those who are close to each other, and how these tensions are either resolved or explode in action, usually of an irrational nature. The tension between father and son in the *Esquire* story, 'The Firstborn Son,' is repeated in the novel with greater detail and more specific results. The tension between father and mother, dealt with in a day's incident in the short story 'The Quarrel,' lurks in caverns of the mind over a long period of time before it finally explodes tragically.

Time is a new and crucial element in the novel. The action stretches over a period of twenty-five years, roughly between the end of the First World War (in the opening incident, one of the two men drowned in the river 'went all through the war without a scratch – Wypres, Verdoon') and the end of the Second World War. In the last section, the Second World War looms up darkly in the background because one of the main characters serves in the armed forces. But Buckler is not interested in chronological or historical time, time that is measured by external events – elections, battles, public disasters. He does glance briefly at a more subtle expression of chronological time, the change in social attitudes. He records briefly and fiercely the effect on the rural community of the spread of urban civilization:

And the people lost their wholeness, the valid stamp of the indigenous ... In their speech (freckled with current phrases of jocularity copied from the radio), and finally in themselves, they became dilute. They were not transmuted from the imperfect thing into the real, but veined with the shaly amalgam of replica.[15]

The changes in social attitudes are accompanied by the physical decay of the original community. Many of the farms have been sold to lumber companies, and the houses have been left to disintegrate slowly, empty and increasingly exposed to the weather. The shadow of time lies heavily upon them. But the orchards, although abandoned, live on. They were 'the essence of absolute ripeness – some niche that time itself had wondrously missed.'[16]

Time as subjective duration, the occasion when it seems to be a servant of human wonder, is never long absent from *The Mountain and the Valley*. Some characters are embedded in time, and life is a dreary battle with it doomed to defeat. For Rachel Gorman, the malicious gossip, 'on no day in their house did the moments move faster or slower. Time was something captive in that room always; something she wore away, bit by slow bit, with each movement of her rocker.'[17] There are, however, magical moments when time seems to withdraw, when, for instance, the Canaan family, under the spell of a Christmas that has just passed and bound closely to the house by a great snowfall, felt as if 'the cable of time had been broken and they were all magically marooned until its strands were spliced together again.'[18] Time withdraws, too, in rare moments of inspiration. Just before he dies, David feels 'as if time were not a movement now, but flat. Like space. Things past or future were not downstream or upstream on a one-way river, but in rooms. They were all on the same level.'[19] Finally, the very old can triumph over time. Ellen, the grandmother, reflects: 'Now years were no longer footholds in the treacherous cliff going up. She had reached the plain.'[20] For her the garments once worn by members of the family, which she braided into strands of a carpet, annihilate time. The garments inspire a sense of immediacy; she lives again the incidents when they were worn.

Behind time, lurks death, mysterious and unpredictable. 'You came nearer and nearer to it, but you could never touch it. It was as strange to the old as to the young.'[21] Many of the deaths in *The Mountain and the Valley* are accidental and unforeseen. They seem to occur as part of the flow of time, not as resolutions of a tangled plot.

But *The Mountain and the Valley* is not simply an expansion in time of some of the short stories. The form in itself gives an amplitude in the writing, a relaxed approach to his material that was denied to him in the short story, especially the kind of short story demanded by magazines concerned about the span of readers' attention. Along with this amplitude and relaxation goes a great change in the nature of the language. The short stories seem to be written in a Hemingwayesque manner, although they eschew typical Hemingway subjects (Buckler had no interest in the manly arts of fishing, hunting, and boxing). But the language is simple, and the sentences are uncomplicated; the complexities hover, as it were, above the surface of the language. But now, in the novel, the language is richer, and the sentences do not yield their full meaning with one reading. The narrative flow is maintained, but it is weighted with description and analysis.

Buckler is still in pursuit of exactness in the use of words that he thought was a goal that Hemingway set himself and effortlessly achieved. But perhaps Hemingway achieved exactness at the expense of complexity and suggestiveness. The world of human emotions did not yield itself to such exactness, particularly when it could be rendered only in words, which were often crude or subject, in context, to sudden change. When you tried to describe an object or an idea clearly and simply, Buckler, again like David, found that it 'fronded suddenly like a million-capillaried chart of the bloodstream.'[22] Still the writer in search of exactness must pursue his impossible goal. For the novelist, the scribe of the inner world, this often meant boldness in the use of words and complexity in syntax.

Given Buckler's strongly intellectual background – his training in mathematics at Dalhousie and his systematic study of philosophy in graduate school at Toronto – he found it congenial to explore language adventurously. In addition, in the last few years of the forties he had been reading widely in contemporary experimental fiction. He had now lost his enthusiasm for American novelists like Jesse Stuart and Joseph Hergesheimer. He retained (and never relinquished) his delight in Hemingway, but Faulkner had now superseded Hemingway as a direct influence. Faulkner too dealt with rural characters, beside whom Buckler's characters had a sheen of sophistication, but they were imbedded in a prose of tortured complexity, which gave them depth and a historical resonance. Buckler summed up his double indebtedness to Hemingway and Faulkner. 'Maybe when I am tempted to write fancy I unconsciously feel the ghost of Hemingway rapping my knuckles; maybe when I get too parenthetical I hear the ghost of Faulkner saying, never mind, that's quite Okay.'[23]

Buckler's novel reading in the late forties was, however, not primarily American. Like David in *The Mountain and the Valley*, he read English novels that 'had more to do with the shadow of thought and feeling which actions cast than with the actions themselves.'[24] The narrator picks out E.M. Forster as an example of the kind of novelist that David especially relished. Buckler himself knew and admired Forster, but the British novelist who most appealed to him was Elizabeth Bowen. Her novels became for him sacred texts. When *The Last September*, first published in 1929, came out in an American edition in 1952, Buckler sent the publisher, Albert Knopf, four pages of specific comment on the text, which he thought had been corrupted by faulty punctuation and by four serious typographical errors. 'How *could* you allow,' he wrote, 'typographical errors to disfigure, if even so slightly, that immaculate prose of Elizabeth Bowen's *The Last September*? It's as if four midgets had been allowed to creep into the anointing oil at the coronation.' He went on to say that 'the subtle and exquisite perfection of her prose delineations ... makes other writing seem like crude cuneiforms struck by a primitive with a broad axe.'[25]

Elizabeth Bowen writes about a world far removed from Buckler's – a world of Anglo-Irish gentry living in big Georgian houses in the country, many of them, like her own Bowen's Court, doomed to dissolution, or intellectuals and professionals living in fashionable parts of London, or in the English countryside. But Buckler's admiration for Elizabeth Bowen arises not from interest in her social and political themes, but in her treatment of the weather, which in her novels becomes a constitutive character. 'I could read a whole book of hers on the weather alone and never lift my eyes. She can get the day and such so right.'[26] Nature, or its changes, as 'weather' suggests, merges with the characters and the mood of a scene in Buckler's novels as in Elizabeth Bowen's. This is the area, for both of them, where language expands in a search for analogies between the outer and the inner. In *The Last September*, a novel that Buckler read just as he was finishing *The Mountain and the Valley*, he would have admired a passage when the young heroine suddenly sees her ancestral home in northern Ireland as dark and desolate, cut off, in the turbulent post–First World War years, from the colourful land around it and from the ancestral beat of the nation.

Only the massed trees – spread like a rug to dull some keenness, break some contact between self and senses perilous to the routine of living – only the trees of the demesne were dark, exhaling darkness. Down among them, dusk would steam up the paths ahead, lie stagnant over the lawns, would mount in the tank of garden, heightening the walls, dulling the borders like a rain of ashes. Dusk would lie where one looked as though it were in one's eyes, as though the fountain of darkness were in one's own perception. Seen from above, the house

in its pit of trees seemed a very reservoir of obscurity; from the doors
one must come out stained with it. And the kitchen smoke, lying
over the vague trees doubtfully, seemed the very fume of living.[27]

In this same novel Elizabeth Bowen writes: 'This good weather
had all the delight of a new perception.' Buckler also emphasizes
the close relationship between weather and human perception.
'In the country the day is the determinant. The work, the
thoughts, the feelings, to match it, follow.'[28] And again: 'The
day ... shaped the climate of the mind as surely as a word or a
smile or a touch.'[29] This would seem to come close to an acceptance of physical determination. But in his treatment of
nature and its changes, Buckler is thinking of its omnipresence
in the country and its fusion with human thoughts and emotions. An example is the scene between David and his father
as they work together clearing a field of rocks. David becomes
more and more bitter as he contemplates his life of drudgery;
his father is conscious of his son's restiveness, but derives assurance from the prospect of the coming of spring. David finds
only desolation in the day:

The breaker drained back. It sucked the voice out of the fields. Last
fall's aftergrass lay withered and matted on the ground. Muddy water
runnelled down the frost holes in the road. A dribble of excrement
stained the white tail feathers of the Leghorns scratching in the wet
sawdust of the dooryard. The boards of the barn were bleached grey.
The sense of touch seemed to leave him completely. It was like a
rainy day when he'd read everything in the house and whenever he
moved his arms or legs he could catch the stale smell of sweat in his
woollen underwear. The day had the sickly smell of scalded chicken
feathers.

Joseph sees a blessed rebirth:

With uneasiness inside, the notes of the outside day struck in him
sharper still: the well brimming clear and cool again, the floating ring
of ice to be lifted out in one piece now and shattered ... the cows

locking their horns languidly, at the lee side of the barn ... the first dry spot in the road presaging dust ... the green grass springing up already in the rake tracks where he's scraped the chips inward around the edge of the dooryard ... the trees bare as the face of someone sleeping, but something soft in the air already brushing against their winter's trance ... '[30]

A common critical assessment that became an automatic repetitiveness in unsympathetic writing about Buckler was that in descriptive passages he overwrote. In the negative report by the reader of the Atlantic Monthly Press, this was a major point: ' ... when the author starts on a description of weather, or the countryside, he froths at the mouth with an uncontrollable spate of words.' It is true that few novels have devoted such a high proportion of the text to description. But it is description that merges with the inner life of the characters. *The Mountain and the Valley* moves forward peacefully by slow changes in the human climate, and that climate is illuminated by the light and colour and shape of the fields, the mountains, and the sky.

Buckler took great delight in his descriptive writing. He wrote to a correspondent that 'catching the "atmosphere of a place" is [my] special talent.'[31] Shortly after *The Mountain and the Valley* was published he wrote to Charles Laughton, whose fame as an actor had been supplemented by popular recordings of familiar classics, suggesting that Laughton read on radio the Christmas sequence from *The Mountain and the Valley*. 'Several American critics have been kind enough to call it the finest ever written on the subject.' (This and a second letter went unanswered.) The long Christmas passage (including the day before and the day after) is the centre-piece of the first section of the novel devoted to David's idyllic childhood. Christmas became a great northern rite in which the central action is the search for the tree, its discovery, and its final transfiguration within the magic confines of the house. In writing about nature, Buckler was passionately involved. But this did not result in a spate of words: actually nature with its contrasts and parallelisms, its forceful domination, acted as a discipline and guide.

The analysis of the human situation often demanded an involuted style, but nature description called for a simple pattern that fell into easy rhythms. Here is a typical descriptive passage. Anna and her sailor husband, spending his last leave together, are about to make the ascent of the mountain, and the prose becomes a quiet, elegiac prologue:

The first grey days of November were past, when the earth lay defeated and colourless and old; and today it was suddenly warm again. Not the sad October warmth, the pale gold hanging in the air of the gently dying afternoons, but like the hopeful spring warmth again. It was Indian Summer.

Pools of dead leaves lay ankle deep in the log road, rusty and dry. The sun was all over in the bright blue sky. It smiled on the needles of the spruces and slid down the pale silver poplars. It settled warm and steady on the dry leaves and the grey rocks. There was a strange sound of stillness about it all. As if the pine needles and the dead leaves and the grey rocks and the clean-smelling brook with the pole bridge they passed over were all singing together a quiet song, like the drowsy hum of wires or of bees. It was as if all the things of the earth were meeting together in reprieve, before each of them died its own separate way.[32]

Nature and human nature merge in the novel, and give to events simple inevitability that seems to lie beyond the artifice of plot. I used to think that this inevitability ceased at the end of chapter 32, with the death of Martha and Joseph. With their death, preceded by Chris's departure to his disastrous marriage, and Anna's new life in Halifax as an adoring wife, the family ceases to exist except in the memory of the grandmother and in David's joyless loyalty to the farm. When I wrote my introduction to the New Canadian Library edition of *The Mountain and the Valley*, I thought of the final six chapters as constituting an anti-climactic postscript. Perhaps the sense of anti-climax arose simply from the powerful impact of the long and loving account of family life that dominates the greater part of the novel. Sinclair Ross, in a letter to Buckler, wrote movingly about the impact. After 'a poignant and beautiful picture of a family, the ties and loyalties and tensions, and above all the silence, it is the measure of your achievement, of the insight and compassion with which you bring your people to life, that its dissolution hurts so much.'[33] But I now think that the final chapters are integral to the book. In those chapters, Buckler returns triumphantly to the family theme. And he is now free to concentrate on David, the hero of the book, in whose fate the reader has a deep concern, particularly because he is the most transparently autobiographical of all the members of the family (Buckler dedicated the book 'to my family, who didn't model for it, but nurtured it none the less'), and presumably the strongest echo of the author's views.

In that same provisional dedication, after the denial that his family modelled for the book, Buckler inserted in brackets, 'nor did I, except as an occasional stand-in'. The 'stand-in' has a career that in many respects is identical with, or runs parallel to, the principal actor. David is the preternaturally gifted child who arouses wonder by his skill with words and numbers. He completes at an early age all the schooling available to him (two years beyond the time taken by Ernest), and then, like Ernest, finishes the pre-college programme by private study. When he is a young man he has a serious accident while helping with farm chores, which leaves him with a perpetual headache and contributes to an increasing sense of isolation. (Buckler agonized about his perpetual headache, never found any satisfactory diagnosis and tended to attribute it to the after effects of his boyhood accident.) In his intellectual life David is a crippled Ernest. He never goes to college, and there is no equivalent of Ernest's summers in Greenwich and his semi-bohemian years in Toronto. Buckler shifts his own interest in writing and his struggles to put his thoughts on paper back to an earlier stage in David's career. At this point, Buckler identifies most completely with his hero, and the novel becomes a deeply felt portrait of the artist as a young man. There was a 'rush of communicativeness from everything he looked at,' and a 'new need to possess these things by describing them exactly in his mind ... And then the whole multiplicity of them clamoured to be known exactly, and so possessed,' but whenever he tried to write, he was faced by 'the never-quite-exactness of the twinning of thing and word.'[34]

But Buckler is at least partially right in saying that he did not model his hero on himself. He knew the dangers of complacent and self-indulgent autobiography. David is viewed ironically and critically. There is a great difference between the David of the early 'Excerpts from Life' and the David of *The Mountain and the Valley*. The early hero is portrayed romantically as a sensitive young man who already at birth has been given 'the legacy of defeat, the strange intangible prophecy in the blood.' In his first love affair, he is the innocent who surrenders to the advances of the woman. The woman is a far different Effie from the shy, delicate Effie of the late novel. She is an embodiment of her mother, Bess. Like her she is opulent and seductive, but her love for David is not merely physical. 'She loved this young, sensitive, mobile boy.' In *The Mountain and the Valley*, David, in his sexual encounters with Effie, is no longer a sensitive and romantic figure. He is aggressive and self-centred, asserting his masculinity and his imagined sophistication. His later affair with Effie's mother is an automatic response that fades rapidly, and he finally embraces a loveless existence.

David the artist is a portrait of defeat. His artistic longings end in fantasies in which he is the magically endowed hero. The only example of his writing that Buckler gives us is a sentimental projection of his own desires. In the final 'vision' on the mountaintop he sees himself as the author of a book that achieves an immediate success. Buckler had good reason to describe the final scene of the novel as 'the crowning point of the whole dramatic irony.' David, he writes, 'achieves one final transport of self-deception.'[35]

Despite what Buckler says, the final scene is not all irony, and David's literary vision is not all self-deception. David finds a solution to a problem that also tortured Ernest. How was it possible to reconcile oneself to a traditional life that had lost much of its savour? Ernest had known a life far more colourful and varied, yet he had returned to his old home, and, despite his recognition of its fatuities and inadequacies, had remained. David's solution to the question was also Ernest's – the sustaining power of a paradise that had once existed. For each of them, it was not just a recollection, but a reality that the mind created. David thus describes the experience:

It is not a memory of that time: there is no echo quality to it. It is something that deliberate memory (with the changed perspective of the years between changing the very object it lights) cannot achieve at all. It is not a returning: you are there for the first time, immediately. No one has been away, nothing has changed – the time or the place or the faces. The years between have been shed. There is an original glow on the faces like on the objects of home. It is like a flash of immortality: nothing behind you is sealed, you can live it again. You can begin again ... [36]

David's final vision rescues his death from brutal finality. He dies an unfulfilled artist, but he experiences the exaltation that precedes creation. Paradise has been lost, but David now knows that the mind can recover it. A mature artist, perhaps Buckler himself, can supply a plot for David's text.

Buckler's American publisher saw *The Mountain and the Valley* as a possible best seller, and arranged for a lengthy immersion in the publicity world of New York. This was to include radio, television, and the press, and Buckler was a guest at two luminous establishments – the Algonquin Hotel and Sardi's restaurant. Ernest was not happy about the proposal and wrote to the office in charge of publicity at Henry Holt: 'I'll do my best not to embarrass you with too flagrant gaucherie. Perhaps we can play it as a sort of Pygmalion, part one.' His interviewers included a great many of the New York journalists and broadcasters who had a national following, Dave Garroway, Harry

Hansen, Charles Rollo (their names and reputations now a little faded). At a luncheon at Sardi's he sat with Eartha Kitt, Uta Hagen, both at the time stars of Broadway hits, and the governor of North Carolina.

In later years Ernest would recall with some wonder this second descent on New York, preceded some thirty-five years before by the young boy's terrified venture into the caverns of Wall Street. The experience had long ceased to have any strong reality for him. He was left only a few comic reflections. He describes his preparation for the trip: 'So I packed my little straw suitcase, boarded out my heifers and leghorns, strapped on my plastic arm garters with the smashing rosettes, and took off.'[37] Only Uta Hagen remained vividly in his memory. Recalling her appearance in a famous play of the sixties, he commented: 'Who's afraid of Uta Hagen?' 'I am, George, I am.' He managed to survive the two weeks in New York, he later confessed, only by going on a steady diet of martinis.

The Mountain and the Valley was not a best seller in the United States. It sold about 7,000 copies – a major sale in Canada at the time, but only a respectable performance in the United States. But the critical success was complete and resounding. The *New York Times* included it in its 'And Bear in Mind' list, reserved for really important books, and the American press, across the entire length of the country, sounded its praise: 'This quietly brilliant first novel,' *Charlotte North Carolina News* (22 November 1952); 'It has all the proportions of stupendous, pounding tragedy, and its characters stand out as though limmed with an etcher's tool,' *Boston Herald* (December 1952); 'Stands with Willa Cather's *My Antonia* or Rolvaag's *Giants of the Earth*,' *Philadelphia Inquirer* (7 December 1952); 'Establishes an author of first rank,' *Library Journal*, New York (1 October 1952).

The Canadian launching was as feeble as the American was robust. Buckler was indignant at his shabby treatment by the Canadian publishers, Clarke, Irwin, who acted as the Canadian agents. He wrote to Arnold Gingrich: 'The goddam publishers (Clarke, Irwin), on top of having brought it out with a lack of promotion which approached the furtive almost, were chronically sold out all through the Christmas trade and have made not the slightest extra effort, then or since, to keep the bookstores supplied.'[38] Enthusiastic Canadian reviewers were some compensation for the studied inertia of Clarke, Irwin. William Arthur Deacon, in the Toronto *Globe and Mail* (20 November 1952), wrote that *The Mountain and the Valley* was 'beautifully written – each word is chiselled with loving care,' and Morgan Powell in the *Montreal Star* gave the book a lengthy review and praised it, although with some reservations.

Buckler had hopes of a British edition. But the two publishing houses that showed some early interest – Secker and Warburg and Andre Deutsch – turned it down, the former with a suggestion in its letter of refusal that such a piece of rough colonial realism was quite unsuited to refined English taste. 'I regret that we should not be interested in your novel, which seems quite unsuitable for publication on our list.'

The Mountain and the Valley had a second and more vigorous life in paperback. It became one of the 'Signet Giants' in the New American Library and sold 150,000 copies. In 1961 it joined McClelland and Stewart's New Canadian Library; in that addition it has sold over 150,000 copies and maintains a steady popularity. Its use in Canadian literature courses, in secondary schools, community colleges, and universities assures it of a continuing sale.

The Mountain and the Valley is the book always associated with Buckler. That is true also of the critical treatment of his work. Regularly in the Canlit journals the text of *The Mountain and the Valley* is painstakingly deconstructed. This critical emphasis has had some unfortunate effects. It was often assumed that he would continue in the same vein, and any departure was looked upon as a deviation from his proper course. But *The Mountain and the Valley* brought to an end the first part of his career. It was, despite his denials, a deeply autobiographical book, and, in the future, he would strive for a wider and more impersonal approach.

CHAPTER FOUR

Charting the Waste Land

The Cruelest Month

The Mountain and the Valley was a book about Buckler's past, recollected in tranquillity. The past was still vividly present to him; the family about which he wrote with such understanding and affection surrounded him – his mother, his sisters, his nephews and nieces – and he was at the centre of it, treasured and loved. For most of the fifties this family pattern was unchanged.

He remained in his home at Centrelea except for visits to his sister Nelly and her husband Harold at West Dalhousie, and his sister Oliver and her husband Raymond Rice who had a small hotel in Weymouth, a short bus trip from Bridgetown. Mona, Ernest's youngest sister, was living in Dartmouth; she, her husband, Bob Simpson, and their three young boys were cherished visitors at Centrelea.

Then, in 1958, the pattern was shattered. Towards the end of that year, Ernest's mother, in her eighty-sixth year, died. There had been a close, happy relationship between mother and son. She symbolized for him the golden associations of his childhood; she had supported him in his determinations to be a writer and had rejoiced in his success; and the puritanical rigidities of the isolated, inward-looking rural society had left no mark on her. She proudly presided over the household and greatly simplified life for her perversely impractical son. There were no acerbities in their relationship. Their life together had something of the friendly, relaxed quality that exists between

Kate and her widower father in the novel he was writing in the fifties, *The Cruelest Month*. 'Two people living together have an island to stand on. Accreted like coral from the little skeletons of their daily intercourse.'[1]

His mother's decline began shortly after our first visit in 1953. The following summer Ernest took her to Halifax for a cataract operation that was fairly successful. It was a long, drawn-out affair and brought his work on his new novel to an abrupt halt.

While things were underway, and all this waiting to see how this was going to turn out and that was going to turn out, it was pretty bad. I spent half my day commuting to and from the hospital from Eastern Passage on buses you just miss and ferries you just miss, and trolleys you just miss, and in waiting rooms which I'm quite sure are the physical incarnation of all things utterly dreary, miserably homesick and worried and not able to find any taste in reading even.[2]

Then in the summer of 1958 his mother had a series of falls, the final one resulting in a broken hip. After a preliminary examination at Middleton Hospital (a few miles up the valley), Ernest accompanied her in an ambulance the hundred miles or so to Halifax. 'The ambulance,' he wrote, 'is the undertaker's and the thoughtful sun of a gorgeous day kept flashing a shadow of just the word "funeral" from the window legend.' But the operation on the hip never took place. Mrs Buckler failed rapidly; during the last few days she was no longer aware of where she was, and was consumed by terror. Ernest described her final hours.

Then I went outside the room for the nurse to fix her up (turning, bathing, etc.) and it was very painful. I could hear her screaming, and the nurse sent the cleaning woman in with the mop that could have been mistaken for a weapon. I was waiting a minute thinking mother might fall asleep as she often did afterwards. I went in and I don't know if she recognized me or not and she died right away and I have the terrible feeling that she might literally have been scared to death and that if I had gone in a minute sooner I might have reassured her

(I almost always could) – and did she die alone and, my God, afraid and feeling deserted ... We must congratulate whoever it is for its superlative technique that thinks of things like broken hips and dementia and fear for the old, mustn't we.[3]

After his mother's death, he wrote: 'But it was a bit of a traumatic experience to have to watch the imposition of that brutal (yet exquisitely refined) and senseless suffering on anyone.'[4]

When in *The Cruelest Month* Kate's father dies in torment after a long illness, her reflections are like Ernest's. But goaded by a cleric's sanctimonious talk 'about a Higher Power's knowing best,' she shapes them with greater savagery: 'I have never liked bullies. If God asks people to be kind to each other, He should set a better example Himself. I'm afraid I must ask you to reserve your comfort, if you don't mind ... until He stops torturing old men to death and burning children in their beds.'[5]

Shortly after his mother's death, Ernest heard the bitter news that Mona and her family would be leaving for Vancouver. 'I'm so discouraged,' he wrote, 'I feel nothing but the feelinglessness, because it might as well be the moon.'[6] The Simpsons were regular visitors, and their arrivals were always joyously recorded in his sketchy journal, otherwise confined to brief jottings on the progress of his books. Mona, closest to him in age, had been his 'twin,' a relationship tenderly recorded in that between Anne and David in *The Mountain and the Valley*. Bobby, the Simpson's oldest son, was Ernest's favourite among his nephews. He is the David in the short story 'The Rebellion of Young David,' and the Peter of the same story that was incorporated with some changes in *The Cruelest Month* – a hauntingly beautiful evocation of the inner life of a sensitive young boy and possibly Buckler's finest story. After the Simpsons left for their new home, Ernest wrote: 'My sister Mona and her family have finally left – it feels like forever – for Vancouver. They came down and took off from here. [A significant move on their part, although it must have given Ernest's grief an exquisite twinge.] I get such gusts of missing them I have to hold on to my hair.'[7]

Something of the mood in *The Cruelest Month* – the sense of the tears in things – derives from the shadow of departures. 'One who speaks of leaving is already half-shadow.'[8] 'The moment of leaving, as it always does, seemed shot with treason, their travelling dress like the badges of it.'[9] The fifties was, for Ernest, a decade of departures.

His mother's death and Mona's move intensified his reclusive habits. But, with no close, immediate ties, he occasionally found relief in a modest social life. It was never a question of his joining an official organization, of, for instance, taking part in local politics (which he liked to observe with the fascination of a disinterested and amused observer), or of becoming active in the church. His social activities were usually informal gatherings that could suddenly blossom on special occasions into lively events. Here are two such affairs, described with gusto but with an underlying sense of comic detachment. The first describes a wedding and its aftermath, and the second a Christmas celebration at the home of his sister Olive and her husband.

The wedding was a whopping success. And a real beauty. It was in that little church just up from Nell's on the way to Ted's. I had thought I needn't worry in the least about my appearance so I shambled out in my grubby old blue rag and the pre-war brogues that I couldn't find a lick of polish for ... and here were all these Italian shoes and extravagant hats and flummery to stagger you. *Neither* the bride's *nor* the groom's usher wanted to claim me for his pews. But Nell had a new outfit with a pyramid hat that scraped the ceiling so I slunk in behind her. I got a cup of tea spilled over my head at the reception and then I simply had to come home. I was supposed to go to Weymouth on the night bus, but decided I was too tired and humiliated. So what happens. I got seduced into a party over at Lloyd's next door, the white house just beyond my barn on the little knollish rise. And didn't get home until a quarter to eight the next morning! It was one of those crazy parties where after awhile someone is in one corner shouting about the relative merits of Glenn Hall's and Plante's goalkeeping and someone is in another corner drooling over someone else and some other two are in another corner having drunk

themselves into what they think are such ecstatically purgative tears ...
I haven't been to one of those foolish parties for ages. And there was
a bride and groom involved and we cutups from the old days took the
slats out of their bed and sprinkled salt between the sheets and all
that ... and after awhile people started dropping away one by one but
the hard core for some reason insisted that I linger and about six
o'clock we started frying bacon and eggs. And here's the pay-off. You
don't know the guy, but there's this guy in the settlement who's
descended from a long line of deacons. So the fire has gone down and
it's bitterly cold and bottles and beer cans are around everywhere on
the disheveled table and I am helping Barbara dry some dishes with
my winter overcoat on, with the collar turned up, and my gloves on,
for God's sake ... and there's this knock at the door and in walks the
deacon, to round them up for a sunrise Easter service! Everyone just
sort of melted away like the snows of yesteryear. Oh, yes, and a big
beautiful cock pheasant strutted past the window just at sunrise. I
tottered home and loaded up with barbiturates and went to bed, but
could only sleep a couple of hours.[10]

Christmas Eve we went to midnight service and arrived late and got
all interwoven with the processional and in the midst of the singing
Ray jumped the gun on the Herald angels and came out with this
resounding 'Hark!' way off-key and about three lines before its place ...
but at least we weren't evicted. Christmas morning we all had to go
sip sherry with a banker and his wife, for God's sake ... his wife kept
worrying that we'd forget the Queen and a dreadful brat crawled up
on my knee, me shaking like an aspen, and insisted on dressing and
undressing her doll in all six of her outfits for my delight ... and then
we had a really fabulous dinner with bucketed Cordon Rouge cham-
pagne and *Hunting* Sherry, for God's sake ... and then we all had a
long Dylan Thomas Uncle-y sleep ... and then descended to Black
Diamond Rum. This went on until I came home on Saturday, wincing
at these dreadful conversations people carry on through a half-opened
bus window with people they're seeing off at the half-hour bus wait
in Annapolis, etc. Many people have been in, bearing fruit cakes and
all. And all the unidentified callers I leave the door locked on. After
they've gone I sneak out and whisk in the cupcakes they've left on

the bench. And I'm only now coming up through the fog a little bit. A very little bit.[11]

As these passages indicate, Ernest was, on festive occasions, an enthusiastic drinker. Daily drinking did become a problem for him in the sixties, especially when it was combined with pill-taking on a large scale in an attempt to combat a perpetual headache and sleepless nights. But even then his mind remained supple and alert. He never became an alcoholic, and could always return to sobriety on his own initiative. He was aware of the fact that he had acquired a reputation for heavy drinking, and resented it. In his letters he had a favourite adage for the subject: 'alcohol is a nice place to visit, but I wouldn't want to live there,' and when the subject of drinking came up, he would say with a touch of surliness: 'Some people seem to think I'm a Canadian version of Malcolm Lowry.'

Buckler was a bachelor by choice, although it was a choice he often regretted. He had elected to devote himself to his art, which was always for him a stern and unrelenting taskmaster and yielded him barely sufficient for his own survival. He was like Paul of *The Cruelest Month.* 'He'd always had to feel that he belonged entirely to himself. The moment real involvement threatened him he would have an instant picture of his own boundaries, map-stained with their own inviolable ink.'[12] But he was not a bachelor recluse. There were many times during our acquaintance when he speculated with apparent seriousness about marriage (although we soon learned not to take these speculations seriously) and throughout his life there was a succession of women any one of whom might have turned these speculations into reality. One of them, writing to him long after their affair was over, commented: 'We all know there've been a dozen girls, besides me, only too willing, but you wouldn't have them.'[13]

When we first met Ernest, he was obviously devoted to Di Lockhart, a devotion that went considerably beyond his indebtedness to her for supplying him with the books he wanted and introducing him to new and stimulating writers. In his journal, immediately after some jubilant references to Di, there is a terse note: 'Wrote letter of abdication to Di.' Perhaps, I speculated, he could not, with his obligations to his mother, think seriously of marriage and had so informed Di. Two years later Ernest told me of her marriage. Many years later she wrote a congratulatory letter about his work, but they never met again.

When after 1956 we began to see Ernest regularly, he would refer frequently to a 'Montreal gal' who came to see him and with whom he corresponded. The correspondence, as I later discovered, was a lengthy and important one. (And writing letters to a wide variety of correspondents was to Ernest a major activity; each letter, although signed with his own personality, was carefully composed, not in the pauses between serious work, but as an essential part of the writer's task.) The first letter to 'Miss Bickley' is dated December 1956, and his last to 'Margaret' on 1 April 1979, just before his health broke down completely and all writing ceased.

The relation began on a high literary level. Margaret wrote to him about *The Mountain and the Valley*, in which enthusiasm for the book was reinforced by sensitive literary references. Ernest could be abrupt with gushing admirers. But Margaret Bickley did not fit into that category. Later she wrote to Ernest that she had 'carried *The Mountain and the Valley* around for a year. Just touching it gave me comfort.'[14] But her first letter was pitched in a more sober key and was largely a perceptive criticism of the novel. He wrote to her:

I appreciate your taking the trouble to let me know that you liked my book, though, more than I can say. No, letters like *that* will never become a commonplace with us. Writing is perhaps the loneliest job in the world and they are its chief reward. It is rare indeed to find someone who understands so exactly what one has tried to say – in whom it sets up such a faithful echo of recognition – and when one does, it's the deepest of satisfactions.[15]

Until 1965 Margaret went to see Ernest regularly at Centrelea, and in that year their love (strong and compelling on her part, hesitant and self-questioning on his) came to a happy climax.[16] But there was a rapid descent from these heights. Margaret's visits ceased. Some years later Ernest wrote to the Kennedys, who had met Margaret, about their relationship. 'We *were* lovers, but, believe me, she's not that kind of "easy" gal. We split simply because I couldn't cope with such a richly cosmopolite background.'[17] Margaret married in 1968, but the correspondence, affectionate and concerned on the part of both, continued. And there was one occasion when Margaret (now Margaret Farmer) and her husband went to see Ernest. In the letter that he wrote to Margaret about the visit, he bubbled over with enthusiasm in his best epistolary style.

It was just great to see you again. I have to admit that beforehand I didn't know how it would go. I didn't really know how I *wanted* it to go even. I was uptight. I meant to show you some of my light verse, but in the swarm of your really being here and my not yet even knowing exactly what I was feeling and how it was, I didn't get around to it. (LIFE AMONG THE GRAFFITI: Nelson kisses sailors / Euclid is a square / Nureyev is uptights / de Milo's not all there. / Little David throws rocks / Luther hurls ink / Tristan swizzles philtres / Oh, what must Descartes think! ... My editor doubts, however, that not more than one in a thousand readers will recognize the allusions, especially the Cogito, ergo sum one.) So I was uptight. And yet, as things so seldom go well when you least expect them to, I thought it went extraordinarily well. Did you? (Editor's note: This man is starting to write very badly indeed. What he meant, of course, to say was: and yet, as is the extremely rare case when things one has expected to turn out maybe disastrously take it in their own hands almost to turn out not far short of ideally well ...) And I found myself surprising myself enjoying myself thoroughly. All right, so maybe I was initially a mite dismayed (a mite?) to find that you'd in effect forgotten me, that I'd left no echoes still vibrating in you, that you found me now simply a likeable stranger instead of the detestable loveable something-or-other ... men don't like to be 'got over' so glibly ... [18]

When she wrote to Buckler, Margaret Bickley was a librarian in the Medical Library at McGill University. She had not reached that position by a smooth, orderly progression through university and professional school. As a girl of seventeen, she had begun her training as a nurse at the Toronto General Hospital (a year before the stipulated admission age for entrance), had then spent the twenties in the vigorous, indispensable, grossly underpaid profession at the same hospital. Because of progressive deafness, she was obliged to give up nursing. She then returned to her home town of Montreal, and during the thirties obtained a bachelor of arts degree (extramurally) at Sir George Williams University (later Concordia) and a bachelor and a master of library science at McGill, working full time while taking her degrees, and supplementing formal work with courses in art and literature. She had made her way by her own efforts, and had, at the same time, endured the stress of family break-up (her parents were separated) and the burden of financial need. Through it all, she had, like Kate in *The Cruelest Month*, that sense of being an exceptional person, 'who would join a circle of her own stature somewhere – the kind of people who cross-pollinated each other with their extraordinariness.'[19] She was not, therefore, overwhelmed by anyone's genius. In a very short time, she was advising Ernest, cautioning him against his extravagances, prescribing a restorative regimen he should follow.

'When I was a nurse,' she wrote to him, 'helping to cure people became such a passion that it never quite left me.'[20] Ernest was not a docile patient. From their meetings, he knew that Margaret had a highly developed sense of humour that could overcome professional sobriety, and in his letters he dealt with his own problems, whether physical or emotional, in a wildly comic manner (stimulated on occasion by alcohol). He thus recounts an examination by his Bridgetown doctor:

A doctor once told me that I had a leaky heart and I've lived on that ever since ... at least I had *that* to cling to ... and Gordon [Mahaney] tells me (ha! ha!, jointly exuberant) that there's not a goddam thing

wrong with my heart. Not a thing in the world. He takes me in to
his machine and shows me that my haemo ... *oh*, no you're not going
to get me to try to spell *that* one, not *tonight* ... is 97.8. Which, he
assures me, is considerably over a pass mark. I urinate in a mug – I
swear, an ordinary picnic mug – and he tells me, and shows me, that
there's not a trace of sugar, not a smidgeon of albumen. Why couldn't
I have had just a teeny weeny bit of albumen? Then when people
asked me how I was I could have said, 'Oh, fine. I have a little albumen
in my urine, but ... ' and then smiled darkly, sort of wispily elegiacally,
so that they'd have got the impression that my urine was absolutely
awash with it, for God's sake, and they'd have shaken their heads
and said, 'So *young*, and so clever ... ' Not a bit. Not a *traaace*. He
says my blood pressure is 180, but (ha ha) we had a great time cackling
over me being such a jitterbug that the mere thought of having my
pressure taken ... And he's sending me for a series of spinal ... cervi-
cal ... I am not! That means the neck! ... and skull x-rays, and we'll
have another big laugh about that.[21]

Margaret was soon of the opinion that Ernest's problems were
partly psychological. His sense of loneliness and melancholy
was the result of suppressed emotions, and he should see a
psychiatrist. Ernest certainly had no intention of seeing a psychiatrist (not, at any rate, a common figure in the Annapolis
Valley). She sent him a succession of popular books on psy-
chiatry. He read them carefully – so he said – and replied that
he

identified like mad all the way. I've discovered that I'm regressive,
anxious, childish, adolescent, adult, optimistic, pessimistic, unrelat-
ing, overimpulsive, unresponsive, penis envying, castration scared,
extroverted, introverted, latently homosexual, masturbating, voyeu-
ristic, clinging, ... battling, oedipustic, fixated, bored, impulsive, restrained, constant, fluctuating, existentialist.[22]

Much of the correspondence is concerned with literary matters, and this is conducted seriously as between equals – equals
in range, interest, and critical confidence. In her association

with Buckler, Margaret became 'an exceptional person' who had joined 'a circle of her own station.' They clashed on some matters. Margaret disliked Hemingway, chiefly on the grounds of his crude masculine set of values, whereas, for Buckler, Hemingway had achieved, by grace, a simplicity and exactness that he himself could only struggle towards. They were in ecstatic agreement on Elizabeth Bowen. In one letter Margaret speaks of rereading *The Death of the Heart* for the fifteenth time, and Ernest, already a devotee, read each new Bowen novel as it came out. (He was shocked that Knopf, publisher simultaneously of *Ox Bells and Fireflies* and Elizabeth Bowen's final novel *Eva Trout*, sold his book at a higher price.)

Margaret's letters were usually accompanied by books – with an emphasis on recent novels that she thought were not yet available in the Annapolis library: Lawrence Durrell's *Justine* and *Baalthazar*, Nabokov's *Lolita*, Cozzens' *By Love Possessed*, Updike's *Rabbit, Run*, Brian Moore's *Judith Hearne*, Iris Murdoch's *The Sandcastle*, Pasternak's *Doctor Zhivago*. She also picked out articles in the *Tamarack Review* and *Canadian Literature* on current Canadian writing, an area with which Ernest was unacquainted (he thought of such publications as incestuous). He was amused by a sentence in an article in *Canadian Literature* in September 1960 by Warren Tallman entitled 'Wolf in the Snow' (later anthologized). 'That the male mountains and the female valley of the title loom up so prominently in the novel is surely a sign, here as with Wordsworth, that natural objects have been endowed with all the seeming numenousness of their inaccessible human equivalents.' 'The fact was,' wrote Buckler, 'that the title simply came from laziness: I happened to be living between mountains, so that was it, numenousness be buggered. If I'd been living by the seashore with a plain running back from it, it would have been '*The Sea and The Plain*.'[23]

Margaret's concern for Ernest's welfare was not always on the high plane of psychological and literary needs. She set out to vary his daily menu, which, if his sisters had not recently replenished his larder, was rigidly spartan, confined largely to simple things that did not require any preparation. At Christmas time Margaret's food packages inclined towards exotica. 'I've been having the strangest meals lately,' he wrote to me, 'cold bologna sandwich, cheeses wrapped in leaves and made from milk taken in the dark of an eclipse by Abyssinian goatherds, and sculpted little puddings with hard sauce and cointreau.'[24]

Ernest was well advanced in the writing of *The Cruelest Month* when Margaret arrived on the scene. Immediately the novel became a major subject in his letters to her (as it was in his correspondence with me), and Margaret was brought in as critic and expert in medical and psychiatric problems. He had come to a pivotal incident in the novel where there is an attempted suicide that results only in a minor flesh wound, but that precipitates the dénouement of the novel. In the context of his story, Ernest needed precise answers to a series of questions: 'Would the particular wound he envisages bleed very much? Could it be patched up satisfactorily without a doctor? Would it heal okay with semi-professional bandaging? Do doctors have to report bullet wounds? Can a doctor recognize a bullet wound anywhere?'[25] After research in the Medical Library literature Margaret had assuring answers to these questions, and to speculations about 'psychological impotence' – a 'cross' that he thought of giving to one of his male characters, a Hemingway borrowing that he eventually abandoned.

Ernest completed the first draft of the novel in September 1958, but because of the long period of inactivity following his mother's death in December 1958, he was not able to submit it to his agent for consideration until January 1960. The agent, Ivan Van Auw, first approached Holt, the firm that had accepted *The Mountain and the Valley* with great enthusiasm when other American publishers had turned it down with sullen certainty. Holt now sat in the seat of the scornful. Their readers (as reported through Ernest's agent) wrote that 'the manuscript doesn't strike me as promising at all.'[26] Ernest, with an infrangible belief in his own genius, replied on 27 January: ' ... I've come to see that it's probably a good thing that Holt did ditch

me. I expect they are looking for a style like Robert Ruark's
and agreeing as I'm afraid I must with *The New Yorker* about
Mr. Ruark, it would be not only quite ridiculous but impossible
for me to try to write like that.'

Despite these brave words, Ernest was depressed. The novel
had been so demanding that he had had no time for short stories
and radio dramas, which had heretofore brought in most of his
income. And he was aware that under any condition he would
need at least another year for revisions – a process for him that
was always slow and tortuous. Margaret, whom I had not yet
met but who knew about my friendship with Ernest, wrote to
me that 'Ernie seems to me to be in a very desperate state
indeed' and raised the possibility of a Canada Council grant.[27]
I wrote to Ernest on 20 January: 'it is terribly important both
for you, and for Canadian literature, that you apply for a Canada
Council grant.' Unfortunately it was too late to apply for a
senior arts fellowship, which had a value of $4,000, but it was
still possible to apply for an arts scholarship with a value of
$2,000. Margaret had warned me that, given his fierce inde-
pendence, he would resent the idea of a Canada Council grant.
He sent her a copy of my letter with his comment. '[The letter]
depressed me profoundly. I spent days trying to refuse his gen-
erosity gracefully, and finally wound up sending him something
he won't be able to make head nor tail of, half-refusing and
half-saying how nice it would be to have $2,000.'[28] What Ernest
wrote to me was this:

Actually, your letter sent me into a bit of a tailspin. I literally paced
back and forth in that excruciating dilemma of being so almost exactly
of two minds about something that you threaten to split apart. The
prospect of two thousand dollars, so that I wouldn't have to leave off
work on the book just when I was really warming up to it, to pot-
boil ... to be free of this sort of perpetual 'coitus interruptus' ... to be
free to wind it up, for good or ill, in a reasonable length of time and
have it off my back ... the prospect of that is pure heaven. But then,
this. This book bites off a good deal more than *The Mountain and
the Valley* chewed. That was, in good part, merely the transubstan-

tiation of the ectoplasm of memory into words. And so, being more ambitious, this one is the kind of book that if it should fall, falls that much harder. So what if I took the Canada Council's money and then the thing were not successful? How would I feel? Mightn't I feel like a robber? And if it were not successful, how could I face *you*, having let down, perhaps dismally, your championing of me?[29]

He followed this passage with long quotations from the novel, and this convinced me that he had great confidence in what he was doing and would most likely make the application. He did make the application, and, as I fully expected, received the award a few months later.

After a year's work on the novel (briefly called *The Cells of Love*), he submitted it again to his agent. Doubleday, considered to be a possible publisher, turned it down, and his agent decided that he must withdraw. Ernest then suggested the possibility of McClelland and Stewart. They had just brought out a new edition of *The Mountain and the Valley*, and were giving the book wide promotion. On 27 July, his agent wrote to Ernest that McClelland and Stewart were keen about the novel. In all likelihood, the keenness about the book reflected the judgment of a McClelland and Stewart editor, John Rackliffe, whose initial letter to Buckler opened with two paragraphs that must have sounded in his inner ear like a triumphal Handelian chorus.

Your manuscript, *The Cells of Love* – it is an astonishing book. It says so much, and feels so much. For the last weeks I have wanted to write you about it, and yet I have felt very hesitant. In fact, I have almost had the feeling that I didn't *quite* want my own thick fingers touching it.

The book is a truly marvellous piece of work. One keeps being hit by it – as one was continually hit by *The Mountain and the Valley*, though the two books are in so many ways utterly different. That is one thing, indeed, that is impressive, this book could not remotely have been predicted or extrapolated from the earlier book. You deserve all kinds of congratulations – and straight praise and applause. And I feel honoured to be among the first to have the good fortune to tender them. It must be – can you relish and appreciate it yet? – a magnificent feeling to have come out on the other side, with a piece of work so rich and so complex.[30]

(Rackliffe never saw the book through to publication. He had uncertain health, spent an increasing amount of time in hospital, and died in the summer of 1966. His withdrawal was a great blow to Buckler, who relied on his critical help – sympathetic, but sharp and detailed.)

The earliest references to the novel that became *The Cruelest Month* are in letters to publishing friends in the United States. After the acceptance of *The Mountain and the Valley*, Buckler wrote to his agent and his publisher about his future plans. To his agent he wrote that he had in mind 'a more sophisticated novel, in the background of Greenwich's Belle Haven district, where I spent a good deal of time working in the 20's.'[31] A few months later, in a letter to his sponsor at Holt, he developed the original concept slightly: ' ... a setting somewhere like Greenwich (which I know very well) with characters more articulate, if not more complicated, than the character of the present book – well-rounded people with a certain urbanity (in the best sense of the word) about their outlook.'[32] The novel that finally developed, after seven years of intense devotion (broken by lengthy periods of agonized withdrawal), was very different from the one he had first adumbrated. The Greenwich and the New York City scene became a brief background sketch for one of the characters; it has none of the depth and richness of Buckler's recollection of his West Dalhousie youth. We are taken on a tour of the famous places that he remembered from his publicity visit in 1952 – Grand Central Station, the Algonquin Hotel, Sardi's restaurant, the Guggenheim (the general American references have a similar tinselly quality – the United States of the forties and fifties evoked by names from the world of entertainment and sport: Rodgers and Hammerstein, Kaltenborn, Gregory Peck, Gene Kelly, Yogi Berra, Victor Borge, Jack Webb). But the slight and superficial treatment of Greenwich and New York City does not mar the novel. For the most part, Buckler has directed his gaze back to familiar territory, to the countryside that had become a part of his life, whose every subtlety he knew and delighted to chronicle, and Greenwich and New York City are phantasmagorical clouds in the distance. 'The well-rounded people with a certain urbanity' – creatures designed for a cheerful and witty comedy – do not enjoy even a shadowy existence. They had disappeared entirely. We have instead a set of perversely angular characters, each obsessed by a sense of bitter deprivation, some of whom echo the thoughts and prejudice of the author.

Buckler had set out to write a novel that would distance him from the world of *The Mountain and the Valley*. The new novel would have a distinctive setting and characters, most of whom could never have wandered into *The Mountain and the Valley*. He would sternly turn away from the seductions of memory and autobiography. But in the long process of creation, both returned, although in transmuted form. The setting remains the countryside he knew and loved, although now married to a genteel and sophisticated life, and the characters and the plot, intricately devised with no overt salute to events in his own life, became a means, nevertheless, of dramatizing his own ideas, tensions, and obsessions.

The moral landscape of *The Cruelest Month* is grey and forbidding with only a few fitful gleams of sunshine. It is presided over for the most part by the remorselessly cynical novelist, Morse Halliday, whose physical appearance proclaims his cast of mind. He has a 'massive leonine head,' his hair is a 'rank crop of animality,' his eyes have 'the jungle glitter of an arab's,' and his smile has no 'true gentleness.'[33] He enunciates his sombrely fatalistic philosophy shortly after he appears, and then develops it in a stream of comment that flows ceaselessly through the novel. 'What identifies people is the kind of thing that happens to them. Not what they instigate themselves, mind you, but what happens to them.'[34] Even Kate, who loves Morse and finally persuades him that his grim fatalism is not always triumphant, subscribes to a stern doctrine. She is a great admirer of Ivy Compton-Burnet (for a while Compton-Burnet displaced Elizabeth Bowen as Buckler's favourite British novelist), and Kate remarks with approval that Ivy Compton-Burnet 'knows that what identifies people is simply the thing that troubles them.'[35]

With these warning signposts firmly established, the real action of the novel begins. It begins with a group of lovers who find themselves in an enchanted place, called Endlaw. Endlaw, an anagram of Walden, a country home turned informal guest house, is a beautiful retreat, somewhere near Annapolis Royal (called 'Granfort' in the novel). It is conceived as a place for quiet contemplation unmarred by the usual vacation diversions. But these 'lovers' – three women and three men – are clearly not actors in a romantic comedy. To begin with, they have said goodby to youth – the youngest is twenty-seven and the oldest is fifty-five. Of the six, two have been married before, two are married to each other, and the remaining two have reached an age where the possibility of marriage has begun to recede. Then each comes bearing a heavy burden from the past; they are, as Morse points out triumphantly, 'amputees.' Still, in this close, romantic setting, love asserts itself, and the novel chronicles its powerful and twisting path.

At Endlaw, love in the pure romantic sense makes one brief appearance. Sheila, the Greenwich socialite, heartily sick of her handsome dolt of a husband whom she has married in a burst of infatuation, falls in love with Bruce Mansfield, a Canadian veteran of the war (the time is 1951), who has left medical school in Halifax to return as a casual worker to his old home (adjacent to Endlaw), to seek solace for his grief at the death of his wife and young son in a car accident. Bruce and Sheila make love in the only concession in the book to explicit physical passion. (Ernest was proud of the passage, but in later years used to speak with contempt of such scenes, suggesting that all novels should have the mandatory love scene or scenes inserted separately at the end of the book to be fitted into the text at the whim of the reader.) But this love quickly fades. Out of pity and motherly concern, Sheila returns to her husband. Paul, the wise, enigmatic owner and host of *Endlaw*, falls in love with Kate, whose devotion to her widower father, a professor at Dalhousie, has meant for her a life of contented isolation. But Paul learns that he suffers from a severe heart complaint that could bring death instantaneously. He decides to abandon his love, to close up Endlaw as a quiet haven, and finds solace in a union with his housekeeper, Letty, a warmhearted, witty (but illiterate) native of the valley. Kate and Morse, attracted to each other, but bitterly at odds over fundamental questions, finally agree to marry.

Throughout the novel, sexual love is always referred to with an accent of disparagement. At the very beginning, Morse sounds the dominating note. He wishes that there was a new word for love, 'one that doesn't pastry-scent every sentence it shows in.'[36] When he tries to express his growing love for Kate, he suddenly breaks off and exclaims: 'I never could write a love scene. Who can? Natalie [a former wife, one of three] said I made all my heroines sound like comfort stations.'[37] Sheila contemplates her 'love' for Rex: 'She had thought so much about love that all at once the whole thing went bad, as handled grief will spoil and stink. Even the words about it that had passed through her mind left that clinging sweet-rot smell in her nostrils, like the meat that has turned sticky in its tight wrappers away from the air.'[38] When Sheila and Bruce first meet and each feels a warm response in the other, Buckler comments: 'And they bent their shoulders to this half-knowledge as if they were slipping into a knapsack.'[39]

At one stage, Buckler decided to abandon the title *The Cruelest Month* in favour of *The Cells of Love*, which, as he explained to John Rackliffe, 'was supposed to cover (in a kind of double, somewhat ironic, application) both the cellular variegation of love and love's sometime poisoning aspects.'[40] Buckler no doubt had in mind also the title of Morse's first book, *Each in His Narrow Cell*. But the main justification for this title was the accuracy with which *The Cells of Love* described a principal theme: '"cells" being used in both senses: elemental constituent and also captivities.'[41]

The reversion to the first title, *The Cruelest Month*, with its Eliot association, was, however, sound, for the enchanted woods of Endlaw turned into a waste land, and the month of April, which, apart from a prologue, contains the entire action, was, like Eliot's, a month of slow and painful reawakening.

April is much more of a constitutive character in *The Cruelest Month* than in Eliot's poem. It is an unusually dry and hot April. The rapid growth has an unnatural hectic quality about it, and at times it seems to echo human despair: when Paul, standing by an open window in the doctor's office, hears for the first time the diagnosis 'angina,' 'a wave-edge of one of those first April breezes that seem to stray with a one-day innocence to the brazenness of towns and cities came through.'[42] The breeze reveals to him the desperate nature of the freedom he had enjoyed and that was now endangered, and, as the breeze died, inspires the most punishing insight 'that he could never escape from the prison he had fashioned for himself.' A few weeks later, Letty, worried by the thought that Paul may be ill, felt 'the same kind of April breeze that had touched Paul so evocatively.' It brings with it a sudden awareness that 'the hodgepodge of reality took no sides at all between green and grime, butterflies and phlegm, spring and death ...'[43]

The confluence of nature, action, and theme is most compelling in the concluding fourth part of the novel. Rex and Sheila travelling in one car, Bruce, Kate, and Morse, each in a separate car, are leaving Endlaw. Their stay had closed suddenly and brutally, with an unnerving game of 'truth' presided over by Morse in his most sadistic vein, followed by a gun wound sustained by Rex as he dallies self-indulgently with thoughts of suicide. Paul, who has decided to close Endlaw, remains behind with Letty. Sheila has returned to her husband, Bruce is returning to resume his medical training, Kate and Morse are leaving to get married the following day. This is, it would seem, an acceptable resolution of all the turmoil of the last few weeks, a temporary peace of mind with most passion spent.

As they drive away from Endlaw, Sheila tells Rex that she is going to have a baby. Rex is overjoyed (unaware of the possibility that the baby may not be his own), and in his excitement throws away his lighted cigarette. The cigarette becomes a small torch, which almost expires until it is nudged by a breeze, another April breeze with a message of disaster, and in a few minutes becomes a raging fire. Sheila, Rex, and Bruce escape the consequences of Rex's carelessness, but Kate and Morse, who have left later, seem to be trapped. Morse, whose thoughts were turned into 'rogue animals' by dangers, refused Kate's plea that they turn back to the safety of Endlaw. He suspects that she is deeply attached to Paul and that return would put an end to their marriage plans. Indeed, in the novel he is now writing about April in Endlaw, he has Paul and Kate happily united. Morse says goodby and moves off in the direction of the fire. Kate follows him in 'a sudden wild centaur of decision.' They pass through the fire unscathed. Morse sees her courage as a proof of devotion, and, in an unusual burst of good feeling, imagines that Rex has also been tested by the fire, has come through nobly, and that he, Sheila, and Bruce are now bound together by the sense of common danger endured and overcome. This perception he will also put into his novel. But Kate, who has constantly argued against his cynical fatalism, sees that this is no triumph for her, but evidence of Morse's blindness to human nature, and a bad omen for the success of their marriage. The fire that began as an ironical accident culminates, not in a triumphant purging of the emotions, but in a double irony of baleful import.

Simultaneously with the fire, nature provides another and surer test of the human condition. Shortly after they leave Endlaw, each of the departing guests see a deer. (A deer, perhaps this same one, had viewed their arrival, but none had then seen it.) The narrative pauses to permit a long and exultant description of the deer – one of the finest pieces of natural description in all of Buckler's work. He wrote to me when he was reworking *The Cruelest Month* about the agonies of the revision – not simply the matter of changing a word or phrase, but a systematic consideration of each word. 'Even if I'm writing about a goddam hackamatack tree, I have to feel what it's like to be a goddam hackamatack tree. The poor man's Stanislavsky. It's dreadfully exhausting.'[44] The deer was much more than 'a goddam hackamatack tree.' It was a magical animal, rarely to be seen when he was growing up, Buckler recalls. In this description we see the deer with a thrilling clarity, and we feel the magic:

A deer standing watching you is the stillest, livingest thing there is. Its very stillness was electric with life, it was framed there in the morning's immaculacy with an airiness of such unearthly grace that it seemed hardly corporeal. It seemed like something her eyes had drawn on the air. It seemed as if the whole morning had been arrested, and forever, in its posture of the moment; like those people in a fairy tale at the moment the spell (or the curse) is cast.

The deer stood there and stood there.

And then just when this whole tableau-fixity had begun to seem infrangible (if nothing had so far caused the deer to move, what in the following life-frozen moments could?), the first test-breath of the wind carried their scent to it. Its head went upward in a flawless exclamation of intentness, to challenge their own. And then, with such exquisitely smooth translation of statue into motion that there wasn't an instant of accommodation one to the other, it was arc-ing across the undergrowth between the road and the treeline as if its feet didn't quite touch the ground between leaps; as sure-pathed as the light and as collisionless through the maze of scraggle.

In one last transcendental parabola, it vaulted a windfall at the treeline and was gone.[45]

The sight of the deer clarifies and transforms Sheila's confused and depressing thoughts. She had a 'vaulting insight,' a 'moment's illumination':

She saw, in this sudden light, the charactered – rather than the caricatured – face of stoicism. It was nothing like the falling in love with her own pain that Morse had predicted. What she saw, instead, was how little, how very little, happiness mattered.

She saw that there would always come a Copernican revolution in your life, when with your weighing eye you saw that happiness, your happiness, was not the earth the sun revolved around – but no more than a tiny planet of no more lustre even to yourself than the planet of another's happiness. That there would always come a time when whosoever's gestures that were now the wands of love, and its bludgeons, would become no more than unaffecting mannerisms. Bruce's no less than Rex's. And that the ones you'd known the longest were by far the most binding.[46]

The sight of the deer has an even more transforming effect on Bruce. It brings him a sudden exacting vision, very much like David's vision on the mountain. But now the vision is not a prologue to death, but to a renewed life.

That was a different time. And deer were scarce here then: a deep woods secret. They never came out into the pastures even. In all his father's years of hunting he'd never caught a glimpse of one. Many moose, but never a deer.

That was a different time in every way. The whole settlement lived in a kind of eternal and unaging present then. The trees and the fields no less than the people. There were no specialized and worldly knowledges to put one man ahead of the other. There was no ghost from the outmoding future then, to cast its shadow on the present and corrode it like a machine. There was no consciousness in anyone or anything, not even in the rocks, of Time's outmoding its very self. All things lived on the plain of a replete and self-renewing now, which stayed as young to the adult as it did to the child.[47]

For Kate and Morse the sight of the deer brings no illumination or vision. Morse automatically becomes the hunter. He followed every leap it made, as it sought to avoid the fire and smoke, 'keeping the cross of our imaginary gun's telescopic sight focussed exactly over its heart.'[48] At first Kate feels a sudden lift of the spirit,

as if her consciousness were challenged to match the deer's challenging grass. Until it came directly opposite. It passed so close that she could see the texture of its eyes and its hair. She saw that its hair was not silken, but coarse. She had from its eyes that trampling look of animals braving their timidity of people in escape from a greater danger.[49]

For both Morse and Kate, then, the sight of the deer arouses forebodings that cast a shadow over the future. The fire has consumed Kate's illusions about Morse. It now fosters illusions in both Paul and Letty, who together having battled and defeated the flames, feel a surge of affection for each other that temporarily translates itself into love. The irony, although meticulously understated, in part as the result of editorial advice, is obvious. Marriage for these two would be a disaster.

The deer becomes a commentator on the action; the fire is an active participant. As befits its role, it is described in greater detail and at far greater length. It too is a classical piece of description, a fusion of Buckler the mathematician, who delights in accuracy and precision, and Buckler the poet, who translates physical into spiritual forces. The fire moves cautiously and uncertainly at first, struggling for life, then acquiring its own demonic personality, moves relentlessly towards its goal.

Rex's cigarette had landed on the platform of a fern that grew up through the alder cuttings. Privately smouldering, it had eaten along itself almost to the end when the breeze nudged it. It brightened for a moment and then fell, dying, onto a dry leaf beneath. The surface of the leaf blackened and crumbled backward as if from the polite and hesitant nibbling of a tiny arc-shaped mouth; but there was no flame. A splash of dew lingering on the leaf nearly halted the arc's advance.

And then a second breeze nudged the leaf against a tuft of dry grass. There was the first little rag of flame. The grass burned itself to death as instantly and absently as an idle thought rising and falling. But where the tip of its flame had reached, a dry alder twig turned red, and a third breeze, almost a gust, following just at the moment when, without it, the twig would have turned black again, the twig began to burn. The gust held it burning just long enough for it to gather its own confidence, to catch the message of fire.

The message began to spread, from dryness to dryness. Little tongues of flame began to speak with fire's voice. Whenever one flame was defeated now by a tuft of green or a patch of dew, there were others to try other paths. Within an hour any one of them was able to defeat the green or moisture in its way. They became surer of themselves, and surer; more purposeful. They cracked open the wood and let its hot hissing soul loose like a nest of snakes. Heat became strong enough to strike blows.

Within another hour, the breeze had become a steady gale. It drove the flames before it with its own surging voice, until they lost their mind completely and charged the woods-line along its whole front with a manic, blazing roar ...[50]

Buckler was aware of the fact that he wrote most easily about nature, with a tendency to overextend where his strength was greatest. In *The Mountain and the Valley*, where so much depended on changes in the outside world, this was a virtue. But in the new novel, nature, except in the climactic chapters, is not obtrusive. The emphasis is on an inner life far more tangled than any he had portrayed in *The Mountain and the Valley*. Writing and revising the new novel became an intense, demanding ordeal. He wrote to Margaret Bickley that 'the first novel I had little trouble in rewriting. The original draft was all in one sentence. But I just went along day by day chopping it up and suturing and any rotten word I didn't throw away I just gave it a little coat of paint and (I'm also an audic) somehow it was at least readable. This one you couldn't decipher with the Rosetta stone.'[51] This was written just when he was returning to his manuscript after a long absence, before the award of the Canada Council scholarship, and reflects (with comic exaggeration) his sense of despair as he began the process of revision. After the award of the Canada Council scholarship, the despair went but the fierce intensity remained. He wrote to me:

I am working very hard on the novel. And to be in the midst of writing a novel is to be living constantly under a kind of enervating cloud. I think you will know what I mean. Its tendrils keep penetrating the interstices of every thought and activity. It springs up with challenge even in my sleep. (Perhaps it would be better if I could manage to take it not quite so intensely, but I can't). However, even if my pace is nothing like a gallop, I am making steady progress on it now, and day by day I wrench a further crystallization of its lineaments from that staggering nebulae of the unformed. And it's a godsend to be able to give it my exclusive concentration.[52]

The contrast he sets up in his letter to Margaret Bickley between the style of *The Mountain and the Valley* and *The Cruelest Month* is accurate (although again exaggerated). In writing the later novel, he could no longer rely on the prompting of memory (the results already stored up in his early sketches). He now had to turn to what he knew first hand (increasingly limited by the life of isolation he had chosen) and to the world of books, increasingly his real world. Now the search for words to convey his meaning, usually successful when he was describing the outside world, become more difficult and thrust him into nests of complexity. He argued that there was no alternative if one were genuinely in search of truth. To his agent, who protested against overwriting, he replied:

I couldn't agree with you more that overwriting is one of the deadly sins. But overwriting is never my intent. I never consciously strain for the fancy or the arresting or the outre or any of that jazz. What I do all the time (although I recognize that in its excesses it can be stultifying too) is try, sometimes for hours over a single arrangement, to find the absolutely accurate phrase for what I have in mind. If it turns out to be an unusual one, I can't help it.[53]

The problems of an elaborate, intellectualized style are at their most intense in Buckler's description of his characters. I complained to him about the difficulty I had in seeing his characters physically, something that had not bothered me, or any other readers I suspect, in *The Mountain and the Valley*. I wrote:

May I make one crude complaint: couldn't you give us some more details, particularly about your women? Kate, for instance, I don't want her chest measurement, or a descant on her behind, but she doesn't exist for me physically, and I don't believe that Paul (who had an eye for a quivering thigh) really fell in love with her.[54]

Buckler replied:

I agree too that I haven't 'embodied' the characters anything like completely enough, physically. But that's a great difficulty for me. It's not that I don't visualize them distinctly, myself. But it's like pulling teeth to have to make them plain to the reader. Weather and landscape and stuff I can go on about forever (it certainly must seem like forever to the reader), but faces, no. In fact, I have such a limited repertoire of feature-description: that I often have to steal from one face and give to the other to make them go around. For instance, I couldn't get any eyes for Rex (whose appearance was really his whole point) so I had to give him Sheila's ('of the blue that can be so arresting when it is as deep as brown') and leave her blind. A similar corneal transplant took place between Kate and Paul. 'The kind of thin-skinned face that the eyes perpetually instruct:' was originally Kate's. In fact, I can't even get the physical picture of a character (except for Papa's) from what someone else writes. I always skip those parts where it's about what they look like, because I know that it would mean absolutely nothing to me, that I'd come through it with no more definite picture of what the author had in *his eye* than that our heroine fell somewhere between Marilyn Monroe and Eleanor Roosevelt. Descriptions should be attempted just the same, however inept; because, without them, characters stay in a kind of insubstantial limbo.[55]

The difficulty that the reader has in envisaging the characters derives in part from their having been constructed from a variety of sources. Morse, for instance, is obviously a version of Hemingway (as Ernest readily admitted) – a bitter disillusioned Hemingway who has left his bracing Midwestern youth behind, a veteran of calamitous marriages, and a writer who has come up against a demoralizing block. He is also a vehicle for Buckler the writer, and in the passage where he describes 'what it was like when a writer wasn't writing' the author's voice lies behind every word.

Did she want to know what that was like ... what it was like when a writer wasn't writing? The solid in you separated from the liquid, to form that paralytic guy sitting on your guts. And then you found they'd cut the cords on the little hammock that held your brain up and your brain had slipped down below your eyes. They'd cut your heel cords too and the hammock strings under your heart and they'd taken the balls out of your voice. The only thing they hadn't cut was the one nerve that smoulders when you watch yourself sitting helpless on your own guts ... You were like one of those days that have no talent – that you try to drink away or sleep away but keep awaking to, dead sober. You couldn't force yourself to write. You could prop the words up on the page, yes; but they wouldn't join hands. You knew the minute you put the paper away each letter in every word dropped down as dead as the spaces between them. That's what it was like when a writer wasn't writing.[56]

Paul and Bruce are also, in part, personal extensions. Paul is a novelist manqué. In his notebook of jottings for a proposed novel, he steals from Buckler's youthful notebook, and his fascinations for word games (our cage/courage, earth/heart) is another authorian fancy. Bruce is the young Buckler who returns from the great world to rediscover his roots in the county. He embraces loneliness, and Sheila reprimands him in words that Margaret might have addressed to Ernest: 'And loneliness is so bad for you. A taste of it does most people good. But you should never touch the stuff. You're like an alcoholic. One taste of it and you can't leave it alone.'[57]

Kate is modelled on Margaret Bickley – an intelligent woman with charm and a delight in self-parody (Margaret Bickley was not happy, however, to have been a model for Kate, and indeed disliked the entire novel). Sheila is Buckler's recollection of a Greenwich socialite, with compensating qualities that raise her above her milieu. In particular she has the ability to make others feel relaxed, to reduce the tensions between the notable and the unnoted, a quality that he recognized and greatly admired in my wife.

The two remaining characters, Letty and Rex, had, as far as I know, no models. Letty sprang vigorous and whole from his affectionate knowledge of dozens of Annapolis Valley worthies, and Rex, the handsome dolt who trades shamelessly on his good looks, is a believable butt for abuse and satire.

The Cruelest Month was not a success. It did not sell well, and the critical reception was sharply divided, roughly between those who thought it was slow-moving and dull, and those who, like David Godfrey (*Tamarack Review*, summer 1965), R.G. Baldwin (*Queen's Quarterly*, summer 1964), and myself (*Dalhousie Review*, winter 1963–4), found it a work of brilliance that didn't quite succeed. Ernest was thoroughly sick of the novel by the time he had finished the long ordeal of revision. He would reflect that had he been able to finish it in the mid-fifties he might have been hailed as 'an angry old man.' Later he recovered his interest in it, and was especially impressed, and at the same time amused, by a graduate thesis that tracked down numerous parallels between his novel and T.S. Eliot's *The Waste Land*. (He had once suggested that his characters could be matched in 'The Burial of the Dead' section of *The Waste Land*, a suggestion that I found puzzling.) *The Cruelest Month* was included in the New Canadian Library in 1967, but it has never been ceremonially admitted to the order of

Canlit, and Buckler the novelist is always associated with *The Mountain and the Valley*.

My own opinion is that *The Cruelest Month* will grow in popularity and critical stature. It is a novel that must be read slowly – and reread – to grasp the effect of its aphoristic, complex prose and to understand its elaborate ironic structure. Buckler, who usually left exegeses of his books to the critics, attempted a summary of *The Cruelest Month*.

I think it was to a great extent a study in illusion. And self-delusion. People think they know themselves; whereas the more intelligent they are the wider they miss the mark. They think they know others – and then they run into a totally inconsistent side of them. That's it: there's no consistency in anything. Always that component of the self-contradictory, the irrational, the accidental – as well as the argon (the only inert gas). The surd. So that you can never add a guy up. Any more than you can add scalene triangles and eucalyptus trees. And this delusion in everything. (Kate finds that when she's tamed Morse's savagery, her great goal, she has gelded him. Paul believes that his marriage to Letty will give him a final peace, too blind to see that the match wouldn't last a fortnight.) Accommodations are made, but most of them have the same fatal flaw.[58]

The Cruelest Month is the waste land of troubled and sensitive people, those that have 'the carillon of nerves that the most significant and illustrative "changes" can be rung on.' And it is a waste land from which there are only narrow and hidden exits.

CHAPTER FIVE

Return to Paradise

Ox Bells and Fireflies

When Buckler finished writing *The Mountain and the Valley* in 1952, he had already mapped his course for the future. In a letter to his agent, he speculated about two books:

Maybe a non-fiction about the myriad, fast-disappearing, unduplicated-anywhere facts of life in a Nova Scotia village as I knew it in my younger days written in the light vein of the old Esquire letter ... or maybe a more sophisticated novel, with a background of Greenwich's Belle Haven district, where I spent a good deal of time working in the 20's.[1]

Of the two projects he envisaged, he decided to begin with the latter, which would mean a sharp imaginative break. The inherent difficulties of the new material were accompanied and exacerbated by domestic crises – his mother's final illness and death, and the departure of his favourite sister. *The Cruelest Month* was very much Margaret's book: she was the model for the heroine (although the heroine was not an attempt at a faithful portrait) and many of the discussions in the book reflected conversations he had with her or subjects he or she had raised in their correspondence. But Margaret was not a reassuring collaborator; she was not flattered to have been the inspiration for Kate, and she disliked the dark, ironic treatment of sexual love.

But now in undertaking the first of his two proposals, Buckler was on solid, familiar ground. He could return to the same store of memories that had nourished *The Mountain and the Valley.*

During the writing of his new book, he was free of immediate financial worries. There were two Canada Council grants of $3,000 each, one in 1964 and one in 1966. He felt that he could abandon book reviewing – work that he enjoyed and did with jewelled perfection, but that gave a poor financial return for the long hours he spent. His letters to me during the writing of the new book (at first called 'Singing as the Farm Was Home') were cheerful. He quoted long passages, which were not followed, as often before, by self-deprecatory comments. On our visits, he volunteered to read passages that he had just written, or rather asked Christine, in whose Celtic lilt he delighted, to read them. This was a departure, for he was usually so eager to hear literary gossip and to raise critical questions that he completely forgot about his own work.

The years in writing *Ox Bells and Fireflies* were unusually untroubled ones. It could always be assumed that his health was poor, but he kept a discreet silence on the subject. There were no local tragedies to haunt his days and nights. And there was a good deal to raise his spirits. For one thing, his long Toronto visit in the fall of 1964.

As I have explained in the first chapter, Ernest was persuaded to abandon his CBC lodging in favour of the University of Toronto's presidential residence in Rosedale. He arrived on 11 September and departed on 8 October – the longest time he had ever spent away from his own home. In his diary, his daily activities in Toronto are recorded with a detail that was notably missing elsewhere. His visit came at a time that recalled to him his arrival as a graduate student at the University of Toronto. This was a time, as he later observed, when the mystique of the place is at its strongest: 'when the dusk first begins to awaken and bestir itself, and the last of the year's leaves drift down so consentingly on to the ground, which is still campus-green.'[2] He explored the campus, searching for familiar places, many of them obliterated in the westward surge of the university, such as the old Trinity House, at the corner of Harbord and St George, 'which suggested,' he recalled, 'a ratty old duchess in a meribou stole,' the digs on Classic Avenue where he had lived during his five years with the Manufacturers Life Insurance Company, and a 'hearty eatery' near the campus 'whose menu proclaimed in block capitals: "This place is kept with unscrupulous cleanliness." ' Another familiar place from the old days, fortunately unscathed, indeed transformed, was the Royal Alexandra Theatre, where his literary ambitions had been vividly dramatized. With Margaret Bickley, in Toronto for a few days, he attended a performance of Jean Anouilh's *Traveller without Luggage.*

He delighted in the alpine serenity of Rosedale. In the evening he would take our poodle, Zephyr, for walks in the neighbourhood. (Zephyr, he said, 'was an ideal companion; he seemed such a well read dog.') On his return from these walks, he would speculate about the enchanted princesses imprisoned in the dark, sombre castles that lined the deserted streets. Under Christine's guidance, he ventured out in the city – to the little art galleries that had not existed in his day (he was especially interested in a William Kurelek show), and to a little theatre, part of an advance guard of little theatres that was shortly to swell into a regiment. He became briefly a solid middle-class Torontonian, going to his club (he accompanied me to a dinner at the Arts and Letters Club) and attending a service (he went with us to Bloor St United Church to hear his old Dalhousie classmate, Ernest Howse). He delighted in the visitors who came to the house – Charles Dunn, a former colleague in the English Department at Toronto, and later professor of Celtic languages and literatures at Harvard, and his wife Pat; my brother Keith, who was contemplating a musical treatment of some of the lyrical passages in Buckler's work, and his wife Clara; broadcaster Max Ferguson (Ernest was to write about Max: 'Here is one Canadian who can puncture pomp and pretension with one flick of his maverick wit, who can turn the staidest situation upside down and reveal its nonsense factor'[3]); Sully Corth, an artist whose studio Christine took him to visit in the Italian section of town (he described it as a perfect setting for *La Bohème*).

Once he ventured out on his own – to see Leonard Brock-ington. I wondered at this acquaintance with a famous Cana-dian, who had become the nation's national orator, and did not find out the story of his friendship with Brockington until I came across the relevant correspondence in his papers. In a letter that he wrote to Mrs Brockington on 9 September 1966, on her husband's death, Ernest explained how their friendship had begun. Like so many of Ernest's friendships, it was sus-tained by correspondence alone, until the meeting in Toronto.

This is how we became acquainted. On D-Day my brother-in-law, Bob Simpson, was a lieutenant on the ship that took him across the Channel. He was beside Bob a good deal of the time, and as soon as he got back to Ottawa he phoned my sister (who, with her small son, was staying here at my village farm) to tell her that Bob had come through the battle safe and sound. This was so typical of his generous and thoughtful nature, and you can imagine what a heavy burden of anxiety his message lifted off our minds. We nearly worshipped him from that day on. I wrote to thank him – and thus began a corre-spondence between us that was one of the most rewarding of my life.

On receiving Ernest's first letter, Brockington realized that he was hearing from no ordinary admirer. He wrote to Ernest, 'I received from you one of the most beautiful letters which has ever been addressed to me.'[4] In the correspondence between the two that followed over the years Ernest reported on his writing and, as was often his custom, explained how persistent health problems had inhibited his career. This was a subject on which Brockington could speak with peculiar authority, and he wrote a bracing rejoinder. 'Don't let physical worries un-duly depress you. Ailments often bring many compensations. I have been badly crippled with arthritis for the last 20-odd years. Eventually nothing fades so quickly as the memory of physical pain. With your spirit and talent, you are bound to succeed.'[5] The meeting with Brockington must have demon-strated to Ernest that these were not simply words of rhetorical exhortation. He wrote to Brockington about their meeting: 'I was immensely entertained and stimulated by your brilliant, witty, and vaulting mind.'[6]

His Toronto visit had been for Ernest a rediscovery of 'the great world': the university where he had first begun to think of himself as a writer and that he could now view from a modest niche on Parnassus; the organizations that were now the main source of his livelihood – the CBC which had given voice to his plays, short stories, and essays, and was contemplating a dramatization of his first novel (Ernest abhorred the private stations. 'Aren't private stations dreadful,' he wrote, 'a wild, dishevelled Marat/Sade of guitars, adenoids, endless commercials end to end, and announcers all of whom have learned their patterns of speech from Punch Imlach'[7]); Maclean's, where he found understanding and acceptance; McClelland and Stewart, becoming his Canadian publisher, where he could expect sympathetic and sensitive treatment. He returned to Centrelea eager to work on the new book that was taking shape in his mind. On his return he wrote to Christine: 'I'm quite sure that my time away did me great good. To get away, whatever one's initial terror, amid different scenes and provocative people somehow gives one a better perspective on oneself – and on one's work. One sees it in clearer outline – from the air, so to speak, and without the myopia of self-jamming.' He added: 'And say that if Calais was engraved on Mary Tudor's heart, 93 Highland is, for quite reverse reasons, engraved on mine.'[8]

A few months later Ernest wrote to me about another sudden, exhilarating expansion of his private world. The immediate source was a visit to Halifax, previously only a routine journey undertaken out of necessity. On this occasion he had met Evelyn Garbary, already a figure in the cultural life of Halifax, who had known a 'great world' where history, legend, and genius commingled, besides which Toronto was an industrious upstart. In describing to me his first meeting with her, he wrote in an unrestrained and breathless style, without a touch of the irony that was usually close to even his staunchest admirations.

She's Welsh and Irish and in her younger days was a real actress. She's played with Olivier, Gielgud, Dame Edith Evans – the lot, and was with the Abbey Players for a long time. She knew Yeats very well and reads him magnificently. Her first husband was Frank O'Connor (do you agree that he's probably one of the most 'perfect' short story writers going, as many do? I don't think I do) and her son by him is with her in Halifax. I really shouldn't say that she was a real actress – she still is: quite unlike so many of these little Neptune upstarts – that indefinable, ineffable voice and presence and flame that if it's ever once there is inextinguishable.'9

How did Evelyn Garbary come to be a resident of Nova Scotia, and a happy and contented one? Ernest's enthralled introduction needs some more detail. Evelyn Bowen was born in Wales. She left Wales in the early twenties when she was seventeen to stay with an aunt in London and pursue her studies in voice, at the London Academy of Music and Dramatic Art. She was chosen by the Old Vic as one of ten young actresses to appear with the company. Then followed two extended tours in the early thirties, the first in England with the Macdona Players in a number of Shaw plays, the second with Sir John Martin Harvey which eventually took her on a cross-Canada tour.

Evelyn met Frank O'Connor in Dublin in 1937. She had been invited by Séan O'Faoláin to play the title role in the Abbey production of his new play *She Had to Do Something*. The invitation came when her marriage to actor Robert Speaight was foundering. (Speaight had left for a tour in the United States and Canada of T.S. Eliot's play *Murder in the Cathedral*, and from America came stories of infidelities to swell an already established reputation.) Dublin would be a happy relief from emotional problems, and the invitation to appear in a world-famous theatre was irresistible. In 1937, the young Irish writer, Frank O'Connor, whose early work had received the commendation of George Russell and William Butler Yeats, had just been invited to join the board of directors of the Abbey Theatre. He had himself turned briefly to drama, and two of his plays were at this time performed at the Abbey. He was enchanted by the young Welsh actress. A brief courtship was

followed by O'Connor's proposal of marriage and her acceptance. They lived together for two years until the divorce with
Speaight was arranged, and then they were married in February
1939, in England.

In the forties the marriage began to come apart. O'Connor
depended on the United States and England for his livelihood.
He found ready acceptance there in magazines and publishing
houses. But now Irish neutrality isolated him from his market,
and, in his own country he was a target for the narrow cen-
sorship law. Evelyn became the main family support: she acted
in radio plays, gave radio talks, and reviewed and wrote scripts.
O'Connor finally got permission to go to England, where he
could count on acceptance and a steady income. There he formed
a liaison with an English girl, by whom he had a child. In 1946
he returned to Ireland, and he and his English mistress and
their child, Evelyn and their three children, and O'Connor's
mother, constituted briefly an impossible ménage. A final divorce settlement was not achieved until 1953.

Evelyn came to Canada in 1956. She had married again, this
time to Abraham Garbary, a Polish Jew who had escaped the
massacres in Warsaw. He had taken a degree in arts, and then
in engineering at Trinity College, Dublin, but, finding no work
in Ireland, decided to emigrate to Canada. There was a brief
stay in Toronto, a city that Evelyn found nightmarishly repel-
lent. Montreal provided a brief respite, but Halifax, where they
came in 1959 and where Garbary got an appointment teaching
mathematics in a secondary school, was, at least for Evelyn, a
happy resolution to their search for a home. Garbary, however,
was restless and, when offered a superior position in Toronto,
decided to return. Evelyn was now employed in the Adult Education Division of the provincial Department of Education and
had begun to acquire a house; she refused to leave. She stayed
in Halifax with Owen, the youngest O'Connor, and two children by Garbary, Richard and David.

In her position in the Nova Scotia Department of Education,
Evelyn had a general responsibility for encouraging artistic activity in the province. This position was given a greater au-

thority when she was appointed 'Artistic Advisor for the Performing and Visual Arts for the Centennial Celebration in the Province of Nova Scotia.' Evelyn gloried in her responsibility. She had a messianic desire to discover and develop writers, especially those who wrote out of an intimate knowledge of folkways and ancestral myths, and had not been bruised by a contact with an imitative urban culture. She was not indifferent to more sophisticated writing, especially when it was rooted in a distinctive way of life. Early in her years in Nova Scotia, she discovered Ernest Buckler, a writer steeped in local customs and traditions, yet writing with a polish and sophistication that aroused associations in her mind with Elizabeth Bowen and William Faulkner.

She had not yet met Buckler when she wrote to him in December 1964 to ask if he would allow a drama workshop she had sponsored to adopt for the theatre his one-act play, *The Stars Look Down*. She had appeared in the radio version of the play and admired it greatly. Buckler gave his consent; he had written it for radio, and, although he thought it an ephemeral piece with a sentimental Christmas appeal, he was pleased that it had attracted the attention of Evelyn Garbary. He had heard about her and was fascinated by the stories of her past. In a parched landscape (Ernest was usually uncharitable about the Nova Scotian literary scene), here was a sudden flowering. When she later wrote inviting him to come to Halifax to see an actual production of his play, Ernest replied in the tone of an unknown commoner who had suddenly been requested to wait upon the Queen. 'Actually I'm terrified of meeting you. With your splendid talent (fine actresses scare the pants off me) your cosmopolitanism – and you knew Yeats! Nevertheless, I'd come if I possibly could.'[10] Evelyn, who was not unmindful of her ability and of the glories of her past, saw herself none the less as one who humbly served the creative genius of the writer. She, too, was apprehensive of the meeting. 'I must confess I'm terrified of meeting you, are you very august?'[11] Ernest did go to Halifax, watched the performance of his play, and then spent a happy evening with Evelyn and a few of her associates that stretched far into the next morning. The presence of Owen gave the occasion a special literary resonance. In his letter of thanks, accompanied by a bouquet of daffodils, Ernest sounded like a troubador addressing his fair mistress:

...Had I known you were enchanting as you are, I'd have been even more tremulous about writing you than I was and would probably never have gone to Halifax at all Thank God I didn't know beforehand. What a splendid evening, in such a splendid company!

You probably have clouds of daffodils on your own place, but may I send you these few from mine? It's a quite selfish move, really. So that if someone one day says: 'I once knew a man who knew Duse' I can say 'The deuce you did! Well I once sent flowers to Garbary.'[12]

This was the beginning of an association which became close and affectionate. In the summer of 1965 Evelyn came to see Ernest at his home, and when, on her appointment later to the staff of Acadia University, she purchased a house in Wolfville (a short drive from Bridgetown), these visits were more frequent. We first met Evelyn during our summer visit in 1967. I recall a gathering on the front lawn of the house on a lovely summer day when Evelyn read aloud a script that Ernest had written for a Christmas cantata that my brother Keith was going to set to music. The script was largely an adaptation from *Ox Bells and Fireflies* (not yet published). There were long passages for a narrator and shorter, lyrical passages that Keith had picked out for musical treatment. The cantata was performed at the Confederation Centre Theatre in Charlottetown in December 1967 as part of a centenary celebration, at the St Lawrence Centre, Toronto, a year later, and subsequently on CBC radio.

Away from each other, Evelyn and Ernest carried on a lively correspondence. When they first met she was spending a good deal of time with a Cape Breton farmer's wife, who was writing stories about the people she had known in her village of Cape Hood. Although she had little formal education, Evelyn thought she wrote about a warm and colourful community with insight and vigour. Evelyn was confident the rapidly expanding manuscript could be turned into a published book, and she enlisted Ernest in the task of revision. Ernest was a sympathetic and meticulous critic, emphasizing in long analyses the need to avoid 'generality and blandness' in her choice of words, and the need to reshape passages so that they moved to a logical conclusion. Evelyn recalls another literary partnership. One of her Centennial year responsibilities was to respond to a wish to present a pageant on the arrival of the blacks in Annapolis County. She found a young poet, David Giffin, who produced a chronicle play called *Coming Here to Stay*, which had its opening in Bridgetown. Evelyn described in a letter to me Ernest's happy collaboration:

I sent a copy [of the play] to Ernest, who thought that young Giffin deserved praise for having caught the rhythm of black speech. Rehearsals were held every Saturday and Sunday through the fall of 1966 and the spring of 1967. Ernest insisted on attending every rehearsal, he made suggestions, which he always followed by saying ... 'Here I am interfering again.' The performers loved him and his suggestions were always made with good humour and with such pleasure that rehearsals almost became parties. He suggested line-changes which I passed on to David Giffin, who agreed with them all. The party which followed our opening performance at Bridgetown High School was held in Ernest's house. The warmth and the happiness of those dear black people seemed to surround him like a cloak, and for a few hours there was no need of protection from insensitive acquaintances, neighbours, or the terrors within his own mind.[13]

Evelyn was soon introduced to Ernest's work in progress, *Ox Bells and Fireflies*. It was a work of great appeal to her – its lyrical tone, its recollection of another and magic age, the 'fine excess' of its language. To one of his periodic bouts of despair, she responded with words of encouragement and insight.

I am not a critic, not learned or anything like that; I only sense ... feel ... often can't explain ... but I know that what you have shown me is as fine as anything you have ever written. You say it is 'ground out' ...

You are perhaps grinding out yourself, but the result is not choked, or scorched, or mangled ... the very essence is there ... it hurts the way Faulkner hurts ... It's like the poetry of life written in prose ... I think writing with this intensity must be full of anguish.[14]

The publication of *Ox Bells and Fireflies* followed a course similar to that of *The Mountain and the Valley* – a preliminary series of sharp rejections, eventually an enthusiastic acceptance, and a lively expectation of popular success. Here the parallel ceases. *Ox Bells and Fireflies*, despite many favourable reviews, did not make an immediate impact and, since appearing as a New Canadian Library paperback, has not, unlike *The Mountain and the Valley*, emerged into a new and robust life.

Buckler completed his rewriting of the book early in 1967, and sent it off to his American agent, Ivan Von Auw. Von Auw wrote on 25 April 1967, damning the book with almost inaudible praise and asking to be relieved of any further responsibility. Buckler demonstrated his usual resilience when confronted with official insensitivity. He asked his agent to send the manuscript to McClelland and Stewart, and arranged for a new American agent. McClelland and Stewart was silent for six months, and in the meantime there were a series of refusals from American publishers: Charles Scribner's, Dodd, Mead & Co., Harcourt Brace. Then on 2 October 1967, McClelland and Stewart accepted the manuscript subject to extensive revisions: the publisher hoped to find an American firm to publish simultaneously (but without making this a condition of its own publication). At the end of December came the glorious news of Knopf's acceptance. This, to Buckler, was like receiving a royal invitation after being snubbed by the court lackeys. Knopf was 'the finest house of all,' the publisher of the great, among them, his adored Elizabeth Bowen.

Buckler was fortunate in his two editors. His editor at Knopf was Angus Cameron, who had been editor-in-chief at Little,

Brown. He had been a victim of the McCarthy inquisition and had subsequently found refuge at Knopf. He wrote to Ernest:

As an old Indiana farm boy your book meant a very great deal to me. There was hardly a passage in it that did not have the shock of recognition ... there are a great many people around who remember a simple world and an even increasing number of people who don't remember it but are interested in it. I think your book is the most evocative book of the lost world.[15]

Barbara Burgess (Mrs Angus Mowat) at McClelland and Stewart struck a more universal note. 'Ox Bells and Fireflies will rest along with two other books on my "perpetual reading shelf" where I go at least once a day for refreshment.'[16]

The book that became Ox Bells and Fireflies was, as I have observed, in Buckler's mind as he was finishing The Mountain and the Valley, and he put his musing into words in a letter to his agent. He wrote later about his concept of the book, now emphasizing 'a straight reportorial account of the "mores" of village life as I've known it here' and pointing out that in such a format, he could range far more widely than he could in the novel, 'describing thousands of intriguing things about ways, and speeches and customs.'[17] It was at this stage to be a relaxed book of humorous reminiscences, with an easy unpretentious element of history and social comment, closer to his articles for Saturday Night than to the acerbic contentiousness of his Esquire letters. A few years later, in speculating about the book, he recalled that he had 'quite a backlog of finished work to tee off from, in the form of long-ago articles (on the remarkable schools I had attended etc.) and, just recently, radio talks (on such subjects as our extraordinary country customs, mail systems, and what not).'[18]

Certainly the book that Buckler wrote ten years later reflects in part the original intention, especially in the central chapters. As he had anticipated, he was able to use material he had already prepared for radio talks. The last part of chapter 9, 'Goose Grease, Death and Parables,' deals with religion and the following chapter, 'Soft Soap and Draw Knives,' is entirely given over to politics, and derived from radio talks. The broadcaster treats religious and political customs sympathetically (but with a suggestion of privileged superiority). These are the chapters that come closest to a survey of the 'mores' of village life. But they are also the chapters where the treatment is light and humorous. Buckler is saying that institutionalized religion and official party politics didn't come close to the real heart of village life. Anglican and Baptist, the two dominating faiths, and Tory and Grit, the two political persuasions, were inherited designations that created little intense feeling except during the few weeks preceding an election. Politics existed completely apart from official party platforms, and theological tenets, ordinarily at icily opposite poles for Anglican and Baptist, were ignored.

Rites of worship were shown the respect of a sober face, but nobody pulled a sanctimonious one. No eye's geniality hardened into the fanatic glitter of the crank. A winter sunset or a hymn might set people half-musing on a Higher Power, but they were not crippled with God-*fearing*. The revivalist's hell-fire singed not a hair. God (when He crossed their mind) was neighbourly. Heaven (when they thought of it) was the green starry pasture of the Heaven on the children's Sunday School cards. The Bible was less a book of sermons (though they knew all the parables by heart) than a great golden country they somehow had a stake in.[19]

The great universals of life were dealt with more seriously, but without a heavy sobriety. Sex, for instance, was not a Hardyesque trap for the young, but a blending of 'comedy and sheet lightning,' with the latter predominant.

As lightning, it is both find and fund. It was the one thread in the weave of life that was all quick-silver. Unlike beauty or any other lure it was the one thing that the flesh, drawn to, could totally possess – in an explosion that turned both people into stars and acmes of themselves.[20]

Death was absorbed into the flow of existence, but was never mocked.

When its great sabled presence came over the rim of Never and took back in its closed hand the breath of someone its hand would never open on again, it struck that stillness of stillnesses inside everyone ... Flesh sought the nearness of other flesh, searching there for the one saving grip: a fellow mortality.[21]

It was a bookless society, and the common speech was often 'the tick tock of empty rote,' or 'a dull rosary of empty shells.' But it could also be a flash of eyelight that showed the whole blood-mesh of feeling behind it.

This clearly is the family and the community of *The Mountain and the Valley*, but now presented free of the demands of narrative, given an untroubled, generalized character. The picture of the community is embedded in passages of lyrical intensity. We see Norstead through the eyes of Mark, the young boy, and it is a world of wonder and beauty. In a winter dream, 'I run to the window and look out at the scattered farmhouses riding the trackless drifts. There is nothing moving anywhere except the smoke curling upward from their chimneys as if each family had just elected a new Pope.'[22] The family, father, mother, son, inhabit a world of trust, understanding, and affection, too deep and secure to be given expression in words.

We walk home together. Father's face looks like I've seen it when the plow would turn up some object of long ago. The shard of an adze or a musket ball that the French or English had used when they were fighting for Port Royal. He'd hold the object in his hand a moment and look far off, as I have since seen men look when they heard a bell toll, the breath of his face suspended. I would want to grasp his hand as if to rescue him from something. But then he would look toward the house, where my mother might be gathering up an apron full of splints from the chipyard to kindle the supper fire, and I would know that we were all safe.

He looks at Mother now. For a moment they look the way they do when they are working in the fields together sowing seeds. When something comes out of them that is neither one of them but more than both. I take both their hands. I have never done this before.[23]

At the end of the book, we return to the world of the child, where each object has its own illuminating glow, and all the sensations merge in one indivisible revelation.

But the rabbits ran in the calm clear moonlight while the children dreamed of brooks and swings, and the wool and the gingham sang warm and cool against the flesh, and the fir trees prayed with the cows on Christmas Eve.

There were cradle hills and sleigh bells. Rainbows and rhubarb. Catkins and robin hop. Locust eyes and chain lightning. Tombstone moss and lilies of the valley. Summertime and suppertime ...

And faces in the doorway and faces in the doorway ...

And there were songs the color of poppies ... and roofs the sound of sleep ... and thoughts the taste of swimming ... and voices the touch of bread ...

And fireflies and freedom ...

And fireflies and freedom.[24]

The child's view spills over into the adult world that dominates the book. The adults feel the sense of the continuous present in which the child lives. 'Time was neither before you nor behind you: you were exactly opposite the present moment.'[25] For the adults too, the natural and the human interpenetrate, so that even the daily routine becomes an act of worship. A husband pauses in his work at noon to eat the simple lunch prepared by his wife. 'At noon he took the bread and tea, sacrament of his wife, on a fallen log. The last crumbs he shook out of his lunch box on the ground. The birds ate them and changed them into wing gloss that will catch the sun as they sing to-morrow on the tombstones.'[26]

The learned professor who became a friend of one of the narrator's favourite rural characters, a woman of 'warmth-wide spirit,' remarked one day to her 'that farming must be a well-high ... holy ... kind of life.' 'It is,' she said, 'Did you ever notice how little it would take to change "acres" into "sacred."?'[27]

Beside the rural paradise is the urban hell. The rural people are whole people who live in harmony with nature and use it to communicate subtly yet powerfully with each other. The urban people are fragmented, imprisoned in their own consciousness, and they are surrounded by unrelated objects.

In the city you walk down the streets with their eyes put out, and noises without voice beat against each other without knowledge. Soulless light strikes daylight in the mouth. The effigies in the shop displays smile their wax smiles ceaselessly against the plate glass. Each face has its window to itself walled up, each with the small world behind it running like clockwork wound up and forgotten. They jostle each other, the eyes only a thing to steer them by. Headless subjects and predicates, no two ever joining to bloodstream a sentence. There is a bleaching yawn of distance between the closest things. The uncreated breaks from its grave at the core of objects and glitteringly prevails.[28]

Buckler was writing in a literary tradition in which the city always appeared as the ultimate waste land, the opposite of the rural idyll, but his brief forays into New York City and the five-year office-bound stay in Toronto gave a personal edge to his version of the pastoral.

A technical device to maintain the ideal, paradisal tone of the book in the midst of anecdotes and speeches that are often broadly comic is the sudden insertion of little glints of memory: embodied in a single word or by a bold collectivity, 'a grief of stones'; by an expanding metaphor, 'roosters, regal as noon'; or by the evocation of a scene, 'The hammock of sunken earth in the grave tops when the rough box collapsed beneath.' Buckler referred to these passages as his 'pointilliste' method. In the first letter that he wrote to me about *Ox Bells and Fireflies*, he filled two and half single-spaced typewritten pages with examples of these pointilliste strokes. I protested against the surfeit of splendour.

I hope that you will weed out a lot of your fine phrases (Hemingway and even Margaret Laurence get by on one or two per chapter; you seem to think that you need three or four every sentence) and let the rhythm of the period rather than the meaning of the word, be your guide, at least some of the time. It's this bloody mathematical incubus that insists on every word = something.[29]

I had prefaced these sharp words with the general comment that the new book 'should be the final and definitive expression of what has been a main source of your literary strength – the rural imagination.' Ernest replied humbly but unrepentedly.

I am very grateful for your remarks about the book. And you are absolutely right, about the 'fine phrases' – or perhaps I should say the 'not-so-fine' phrases. (When are you not right?) They're like rhinestones on street dress. But if I take them out what will I have left? They're all I've got! And they're like dragon's teeth. When I yank one out two spring up in its place. No, I will try to weed them out. On my knees, praying that they will not return. And I'll try to curb the mathematical thing, the 'equals' obsession.[30]

Ox Bells and Fireflies was, in one sense, an impersonal structure: the narrator hovers indistinctly in the background; every character and every incident is representational, and there is no narrative line. In another sense, it is the most personal of Buckler's books. 'I really squeezed my heart into this book,' he wrote to Barbara Hutchinson, an editor for McClelland and Stewart.

Ox Bells and Fireflies is a celebration of the qualities that Buckler most admired – selflessness, integrity, kindness, love. He uses a series of portraits and occasional narratives that are simple, cogent, and unsentimental. These are not essays in virtue. 'No one could pretend that every Norsteader was a blood ruby, or holy with that holiness of the unperjurable that bread baked by a wood fire has, or gold.' Buckler was aware of the 'grimy underpelt' of everything ('what Beckett had wrought,' he would say), and he conveniently concentrated his dark view in another fictional village, where 'talk was the dry, dry, raisins of the grapes of talk,' where religion 'parched and puckered them like chokecherry juice,' and 'laughter sounded like sandpaper on glass.'[31]

Perhaps Norstead never existed, or existed only in the pure consciousness of Buckler, the child. But to Buckler, in his isolation and awareness of corroding change, its resurrection was a necessity and his salvation. Two of his characters – David in *The Mountain and the Valley* and Bruce in *The Cruelest Month* – had had a vision of the old, idyllic life, but it had been sudden and transitory. Now Buckler would give substance to their vision; he would supply a detailed plot for their text. He would invoke not memory, but the heart.

The heart is far less misty-eyed than the mind ... once in a while it leaps of its own accord – through the skin, through the flesh, through the bone – straight back to the pulse of another time, and takes all of you with it. You are not seeing this place again through the blurred telescope of the mind: You are standing right there. Not long enough to take it all down, but long enough to give memory a second chance.[32]

A particular place would, in Buckler's vision, expand into a timeless universe:

I've tried to underline the omnipresence of the far in the near (maps of Tasmania on the cow's brockled sides); the universal in the particular (all geometry in the owl's eye); the macrocosm in the microcosm (whole galaxies in a pasture of wildflowers); the duplicate rendering of every mood in some physical object or cast of nature (all sadness in the swinging of an unhinged November gate); the infinite clusters of varying determinants of behaviour in the infinite variants of weather or season: the translatability of the senses one into another (songs the color of poppies, roofs the sound of sleep ...) The interlocking and cross-pollination of all things, tangible or intangible. And especially a celebration of these senses. With particular attention to those 'fireflies' of pure joy which so often grazed the villager's consciousness in work or play (no fretful whimpers about 'absurdity' or 'alienation' then, no winkling out of hung-up psyche with a crochet hook) while the faculty of wonder was still intact.'[33]

Ox Bells and Fireflies is the charting of a paradise that David and Bruce had each glimpsed for a brief ecstatic moment. It is written with the uncompromising exactitude of poetry. After two versions of Paradise Lost, Buckler in Ox Bells and Fireflies wrote his Paradise Regained.

CHAPTER SIX

Man of Letters

With the publication of *Ox Bells and Fireflies* in 1968, Buckler completed his major undertaking. Each of the three books he had written had been profoundly personal. They had grown out of his own experience and his deepest convictions, and they had been shaped over a long period with disciplined devotion. Each was different from the other, but the three were bound together, so that they formed a trilogy. *The Mountain and the Valley* is about a paradisal rural society to which the passage of time brings change and decay. In this society, the artist is a stranger, to some extent an outcast, and he suffers isolation and dies, young and unfulfilled. The *Cruelest Month* is about an urban, sophisticated society, temporarily shifted to a rural setting, in which the burden of the past brings time to a halt. Here the artist is a satanic figure who attempts to subdue life to his own private vision. In *Ox Bells and Fireflies*, Buckler returns to his rural paradise, now happily enmeshed in a timeless world. The narrator is the artist, no longer objective and ironic, as in the first two books, but a participant and interpreter, for whom all nature is an illuminating parable.

For the ten years that remained to Buckler as an active writer, he ceased to be the possessed artist and retreated to the role of the professional who could respond effectively to suggestions or remake occasional work from the past. The change came as the result of his own sense of having completed a major enterprise and from an imaginative exhaustion—from 1968 onward he often complained that he couldn't get hold of an idea for a book. But the disciplined professional, the uncompromising stylist, the sharp critic both of his own work and work of others remains to the end.

Nova Scotia: Window on the Sea was the first of the three books of the seventies to be published. (It appeared in 1973; *Whirligig* in 1977. The collection of short stories, *The Rebellion of Young David*, appeared in 1975, but it was a collection of work done entirely in the past.) The original idea for *Window on the Sea* came from the photographer with whom Ernest collaborated. Hans Weber was a young German living in the United States who had enrolled at Acadia University and was a student in Evelyn Garbary's class in creative writing. Evelyn finally succeeded in persuading Ernest to attend one of her classes where he delighted the students by his easy professional authority and his deep interest in their work. Hans was especially enthralled. He speculated about taking a house close to Ernest and studying writing under his direction. But Hans' primary interest was in photography, in which he had already gained some recognition. In June 1969, Ernest wrote in a letter about the visit of an Acadia student, 'a professional photographer on the side, taking atmospheric shots of everything around including me, for a proposed picture book of N.S.'[1] Hans talked to Ernest about his writing a prose accompaniment in the style of *Ox Bells and Fireflies*. The enterprising Hans went to see McClelland and Stewart about the book. They showed an interest, stimulated by the prospect of the Buckler contribution (Jack McClelland, the publisher, had been enchanted by *Ox Bells and Fireflies*, and saw Buckler as a valuable 'property' to which he was eager to link the McClelland and Stewart name). Pamela Fry, a McClelland and Stewart editor, came down in March 1970 to plan the book. Ernest wrote to me:

I plugged hard for using 'adapted' text from *Ox Bells*, but no sale. They want something fresh. They consider Hans a 'real find' and prophesy that the two of us will put the old province on the map. But what have I left fresh to say about Nova Scotia? I'm scared. In truth, I'm terribly scared of this whole crazy, topsy-turvy violent world that I don't seem to belong in.[2]

Ernest never struck me as a fervent Nova Scotian. His region was a small area in the Annapolis Valley, a narrow band stretching from Bridgetown in the north to Digby in the south, and even most of this area was outside the range of his books. Halifax was a separate extension of his little kingdom, a city blessedly separated in his mind from the general urban waste land 'where the myth-softened mask of a history which has been unique as nowhere else pervades even the impervious.'[3] But he had no first-hand knowledge of the rest of the province, and he had never been to Cape Breton. (When I showed him some coloured slides that I had taken of Cape Breton, he responded with delight and astonishment, as if he had just been introduced to a fabulous and distant island.) He felt no kinship with fellow writers from Nova Scotia except for Alden Nowlan. ('When Nowlan shifts from poetry to prose, the poetic gift does not translate into lint; it is simply the extra eye which sees through things to the core,' he wrote in a review of Nowlan's *The Glass Roses*.) In *Window on the Sea*, however, he permitted himself a few rhapsodic passages about the province, conscious as a professional writer that in such a book this was an obligatory exercise. Yet these passages of generalized praise are not strident; the sweeping statements have a quiet, self-assured eloquence. 'Nova Scotia is ... nearly the last place left where place and people are not thinned and adulterated with graftings that grow across the grain.'[4] I can think of only one place where a deeply felt generality becomes rhetoric. 'Nova Scotia is the face from Genesis and the face from Ruth. The face from Greco and the face from Rubens. The life from Faulkner and the life from Hardy) ... '[5] (When I was searching in *Window on the Sea* for a laudatory passage on Nova Scotia to adorn a convocation speech at Dalhousie University, this was the only passage that had the requisite rhetorical ring.)

If *Window on the Sea* is a celebration of Nova Scotia, it is a far cry from the coffee-table book that it resembles in size and format. The prose dominates although it takes up only 40 of the 127 pages. It does not explain or comment on the pictures. It exists in its own right, and the pictures are an atmospheric background for the prose. The pictures are sardonic comments on the conventional coffee-table book: small, care-worn houses instead of Victorian mansions; studies of familiar objects instead of broad vistas of field, sea, and sky; close-ups of humble workers on land or sea instead of (to use Buckler's words) 'nubile gals bounding out of the Chamber-of-Commerce surf with breasts the skimpy bikini bras can barely restrain.'

In *Windows on the Sea*, Buckler's approach to his subject is the same as it was for *Ox Bells and Fireflies*. Indeed the new book is, in a sense, a completion of the earlier one – an expansion of the imaginary village of Norstead into the whole of Nova Scotia. The technique of presentation is the same. The solid expository prose is broken by gatherings of minute observations of particulars ('amethysts in the imperial rocks at Blomidon,' 'the dragonfly rising from the landlocked brook'), what Buckler calls his 'pointilliste' technique; by short snatches of dialogue; and by isolated incidents in the life of the Nova Scotians that are designed to be representational, to summon up associations and memories. In the centre is a complete short story that had been written several years before, and that Buckler had considered developing into a novel. His justification for its use was that it was 'a shifting of glass,' a relief for the reader, a contrast in its simple, direct style and easy narrative flow, from the complex prose of the surrounding sections. But the story has also an integral role in the book.

'Man and Snowman' is a superb story in itself, one of Buckler's best, and it reinforces the rest of the text at the same time that it provides a contrast. An elderly Nova Scotian, one of Ernest's mutely heroic figures, is a hopeless invalid as the result of a stroke, confined to his bed and incapable of speech. As he lies in his bed he recovers in his mind the experiences of his past – boyhood, youth, marriage, a spell in the city, the death of his wife, and the subsequent years of gradual recovery from the blow. His memory moves in units of five years and, as the story opens, he is trying desperately to reach seventy, which he thinks must have been an eminence from which he could observe his past. But he cannot reach the plateau. Outside his grandchildren are playing in the snow, building snow forts and a snowman. Through the window he can see them clearly. Overnight the snow forts and the snowman dissolve in an early rain. In the morning his son finds him dead. We learn that he has not reached seventy. The slate that he has used to express occasional direction or response has one word that is difficult to puzzle out. The grandson who has been closest to him finally deciphers it; it is 'peace.'

The mood of the story – lyrically elegiac – is the mood of the book as a whole. The principal character exemplifies the fortitude and integrity that Buckler sees as Nova Scotian virtues, and the picture of the family – son and daughter who care for the invalid with love and devotion, grandchildren who see their grandfather still alive and vital – has the quality of an unsentimental idyll. The story deals with sorrow and death, but both become part of the texture of life. 'Here, starker than anywhere else, are the reminders of how inexorably one's address shifts from the letter to the tombstone; of what useless armour is the scarecrow, thought, against the crows of Time.'[6]

The prose of the four expository sections is complex and demanding. He wrote to his editor, Pamela Fry: 'I tried to make the text as succinct as possible. Think it should be almost as dense (in the sense that doesn't mean "stupid") as poetry. Would spend a day over one line sometimes to get this kind of compactness.'[7] The poetic intensity of the prose arises, as in *Ox Bells and Fireflies*, from the attempt to render the complex world in which Buckler's ideal Nova Scotian lives, an instantaneous translation that goes on in his mind between the inner and the outer, the elevation of the particular into the universal.

And what any account of them must recurrently come back to is the constant interplay of their senses with what is everlastingly intrinsic and near; until finally they come as if to have a common bloodstream with it. A current that puts them in the presence, at least, of all the vastnesses of implication in each particle (each a universe) that surrounds them. This, if not in their head, is in their bones, in instance after instance.[8]

Buckler is writing here not only of an aesthetic response but a moral quality. What he is describing belongs to the heart and not to the mind. Nova Scotia is itself a heartland: 'what saves it from insularity is a peninsularity like that of the heart. The arteries go out to the Main, but the beat is all of itself.'[9] And later (with an assist from mathematics):

Nova Scotia has no linear equalities within itself, but (taking the sea as base) it forms an isosceles triangle with the man who loves it, welding him, where their equal sides converge, to the universals ... of nowhere can it be said with more truth that here is where the heart meets its match in every sense of the word.[10]

The 'heart' for Buckler is the imagination in action binding one man to another, clarifying the fundamentals. It enables man to live close to mortality and see it as part of the mainstream of life. 'Even the ghosts of the drowned have a quality of sincerity and deathlessness about them that no others of the dead do.'[11] There is an element of fierce moralism in the writing here as if Buckler were trying to erect Nova Scotia into a barrier against the modern world he increasingly hated, where 'the advance spy of Babel and steel, has already begun to infiltrate and infest the land, begun to shoulder its individuality aside and mark it out for parcelment, and where "television" aerials comb the night for dross or screams.'[12] In his answer to the inevitable questionnaire from his American publisher, Crown, the joint publisher with McClelland and Stewart, he concluded his '300 word description of your book,' with these passionate words: 'but here the windmills of the heart still turn truthfully in the clear breeze. That's what I'm dying to record, before I die or it does.'

Although *Whirligig* came out after *Window on the Sea*, its origins are earlier, with no indebtedness to external prompting.

Buckler thought of it as a book that would emphasize personal qualities not given expression in his first three books. He recalled the *Esquire* letters in which the youthful Buckler had been a venomously effective critic who was read with delight. He had not abandoned the role of critic and satirist (shading into humorist), as his correspondence richly attests. In part, this was a means of containing and subduing his own fits of despondency and his chronic ill health. Margaret Laurence wrote to him: 'For someone who knows much more profoundly than I do, what I mean when I say "The Black Celt" within, you write the most stubbornly witty letters I have ever read. Don't think I don't know how valuable this survival humour is, Ernie, – I really do.'[13]

The 'survival humour' was crucial for the artist. He wrote to Christine and me about a series of problems with *Window on the Sea* and with what he called his 'funny book':

The text of the 'picture book' of Nova Scotia lags, with deadlines pressing, and sometimes I get so goddam depressed I could walk under an ordinary depression like a limbo dancer. But I guess that melancholia is the writer's occupational disease, and that he can only hope that he'll be given a happier job in Heaven than the one he's stuck himself with here. To add to it all, I lost (as I think I told you) a large section of the 'funny' stuff, and also, somewhere I think on the bus from here to Evelyn's, a crucial section of the picture book. Though hardly comparable to the arson of Carlyle's 'French Revolution' at the maid's torch, very disheartening nevertheless.[14]

Humour, often with a bitter flavour, was a barrier against an immediate environment that he occasionally found repugnant. In thanking us for a Christmas record, he wrote:

I want to thank you for Marat/Sade. An astonishing, somewhat scarifying but plungingly stabby play. I suppose that 'enjoyed' is not quite the accurate word for my reaction to it, but it certainly stirs up the somnolent sediment in the pool of one's consciousness to a really vivifying, rolling boil. I think I've been thinking sharper ever since I heard it. About as sentimental as a sword, it yet shows what heart-to-heart 'recognitions' a virtuosic use of the human voice can accomplish. (I am thinking seriously of putting on the play here next June at the Apple Blossom Festival, to follow what the Directors of this horrendous event still persist in calling 'semi-religious concerts.' The casting would be easy. There are thousands of perfect lunatics within a stone's throw who would superbly qualify. I haven't decided yet whether I'll play Marat or Sade. I'm for goddam sure not at my handsomest in a bathtub.[15]

In the seventies Ernest became more and more concerned about his health. But even an account of an intensive check-up in the Lahey Clinic in Boston, followed by an operation at the associated Brooks Hospital, was the occasion for an extended comic extravaganza:

Battle dress at the Brooks is a sort of see-through Johnny Shirt that out-minies anything I've ever seen, with the Southern exposure of course entirely 'naked to mine enemas.' At the Lahey itself, the garb is something else. For men and women both, a sort of flour-bag peignoir that nearly reaches the ground, with at the top what I think is called a 'princess' neckline, and some intricate cross-lacing which constitutes a charming bodice. All very decorous – except when you cross your legs. Then the whole nether section of this drapery springs wide apart and you are (inadvertently) a far more flagrant exhibitionist than Dietrich ever was in her split-level Balaanciega.[16]

When we visited Ernest, it was always the humorist and the satirist who dominated. The laughter began as soon as we arrived, and continued intermittently until we began our preparations for departure when Ernest would suddenly fall silent. When he first mentioned the possibility of writing a 'funny book,' I rejoiced. It would be the answer to the question that always haunted him even as he was still in the midst of a major project; 'What can I do next?' And he would be turning to a fresh subject in which at the same time he had demonstrated a natural ability. I wrote to him about a lecture on 'Mark Twain and Leacock' that I was giving during my tenure of the chair of Canadian studies at Harvard, 1967–8, and he wrote in reply:

I was most interested to hear about your main lecture on Leacock and Twain. (I've been thinking, myself, about letting the metaphysical verities stew in their own dry juice and trying to turn myself into a funny man for awhile.) And of course the humorist is the prime social critic. Or used to be, anyway. (Nowadays, the fact of things is itself so ludicrous that it is its own attack and leaves the humorist or satirist almost nowhere to go.) You didn't mention Twain's 'Letters From God' (I'm not sure if that's the exact title), but I'm sure you must have read it. I don't think it was published until recently, but there is the man not only in his comic vein but in all his biliar majesty. I've always felt that at times Leacock was, in his humour, a trifle 'vicarish' or 'naughty,' but, by God, he gets many an arrow home too.[17]

The book that finally emerged nine years later was not the book I envisaged, or, I suspect, that Buckler envisaged. *Window on the Sea* took up three years, and by then Ernest was exhausted and incapable of sustained work. He had taken to writing light verse in the manner of Ogden Nash (but with only an occasional recall of the master), an exercise adjusted to the increasingly short period during which he could concentrate on literary matters. A great deal of the prose that was included in *Whirligig* (initially called 'Hamlet, or Oh Dad, Poor Dad, I'm Hung Up in Ma's Closet and I'm Feeling So Sad') had been written before and never published, so that the book became a collection of miscellaneous material and had no unifying idea. The book was long in gestation. Jack McClelland was not initially enthusiastic, and insisted on additional fresh material that Buckler found difficult to furnish.

The point of view shifted from piece to piece. Sometimes it is that of the farmer who writes in his spare time but is always conscious that his neighbours think of writing as a frivolous activity. Occasionally he is a well-read philistine who ridicules the opera and avant-garde writing. In one piece, he is a literary critic who confines himself to non-qualitative judgments about what makes a best seller; and in another he is an amateur sociologist who examines rural ways and, in his most adventurous role, he is a husband who must show authority in the household. Buckler could be sympathetic with all these roles without identifying with any of them. The book has a light and cheerful tone; the humour is directed against relatively innocent activities: advertising, the ritual of Christmas cards, cultural pretentiousness. More serious subjects are handed over to verse – religious tolerance and extremism, woman's lib, or sexual explicitness. This subject inspired a classical limerick, in which the concluding line combines surprise, inevitability, and verbal wit:

> Stage antics are getting so bold,
> That the 'act' will soon follow, we're told
> But where is the actor
> With enough vital factor
> To play eight weeks and not fold?

But limericks and prosy lines punctuated by sudden elaborate rhymes are not good vehicles for satiric indignation.

My favourite piece is called 'It's not the thought, it's the card.' Dorothy Parker said of the humorist that 'he has a disciplined eye and a wild mind,' and Buckler's piece bears out this cogent definition. Only a disciplined eye could describe the simple facts with such accuracy, and only a wild mind could devise a response so fantastically logical. Here is the opening section of the piece:

Let's face it – the chief concern in the matter of Christmas cards is to hit on a parity as exact as possible between the one you send and the one you get. What bugs you more than to send Al and Gertie a twenty-cent card, sealed, with a long chatty note (outlining among other things your dreadful siege with a ruptured disc), and get back a sleazy nickel job, unsealed and bearing the casual scrawl, 'Do hope you are well'? My wife and I have taken a hard-headed look at this problem and I feel like passing along the scientific method we came up with, for what it's worth.

Last year we rated each card as received, on a point basis. Feature by feature. Our ratings may not be yours, of course ...

There then follows a rating of each Christmas card based on its probable cost, whether it is sealed or unsealed, and whether it contains (a) a note and (b) a snapshot, each of 'a' and 'b' being down-rated if it is 'a plain between-the-lines boast of how the sender's status symbols have mushroomed during the past year.'[18] Both *Window on the Sea* and *Whirligig* sold well in Nova Scotia, but languished elsewhere. Buckler had the impression that McClelland and Stewart had little interest in *Whirligig* and had not bothered to publicize it. He noted, however, that it had the enthusiastic endorsement of Don Harron, himself a humorous writer of note, who praised it on the influential radio program, *Morningside*. It won the Leacock medal for humorous writing (like most Canadian literary medals, gilded modestly with a cash prize). Buckler was unable to attend the award dinner in Orillia, and asked that I accept the award on his behalf. From my notes for the occasion, I extract the following (still valid, I think, despite the after-dinner rhetoric):

Whirligig is a book very close to Buckler, one that he had to write, for the humorist has always lived close to the poet, the writer who could probe the human heart has always been fascinated by the elaborate facades with which human beings confront each other.

In recent years his health has not been good, and he found it quite impossible to come here for this event. He is a person of extraordinary sensitivity: he lives, as he writes, with an almost agonizing awareness of emotions and feelings. But there is always the saving core of humour, a balancing force, an emotional release, the other side of beauty and wonder, and sometimes closely related to them.

On your behalf, I salute Ernest Buckler, for whom, as for all great writers, the world is both beautiful and absurd, tragic and comic, where ox bells and fireflies exist in a timeless valley, and where bores, pedants, and clowns are perpetually caught up in a mad and colourful whirligig.

The fifties and sixties had been Buckler's productive decades as a writer. The seventies were the decade when his achievement was recognized. Three major Maritime universities awarded him honorary degrees, the University of New Brunswick in 1969, Dalhousie in 1971, and Acadia in 1978. He was grateful for the recognition, but his natural disposition was, if at all possible, to avoid the official ceremonies. UNB granted the degree in absentia, but Dalhousie and Acadia held to the usual academic rule that the honorary graduand must attend the ceremony in person. Buckler accepted the condition and presented himself at both Dalhousie and Acadia. Neither was the ordeal he had ruefully anticipated. Indeed at Dalhousie he greatly enjoyed the whole affair. He reported that he 'tried to look like Essex in the squashy hat, but failed utterly.' He liked his fellow honorary graduands. 'Isaac Stern, the violinist, was no trouble ["what do I say to a violinist," he had speculated, "Keep your chin up?"], and I had a long talk with his wife who is a dandy gal. John Gray, President of Macmillan's, was easy, and I liked Grossman (Director of Vancouver Public City Library).'[19]

The nation (as embodied in the Order of Canada) also recognized Buckler's distinction. In January 1974, he was appointed a member of the order, and commanded to appear at Rideau Hall on 16 April to receive the insignia. A trip to Ottawa was out of the question. A few months before, he had returned from the Lahey Clinic in Boston after some surgery with advice to prepare for another visit and, in all likelihood, further surgery. He was none the less anxious to receive the award in the offical manner, from the head of state, the governor-general. He was, in a mild, non-exclamatory way, a monarchist, and he set store on a ceremony presided over by the queen's representative. To his great delight, special arrangements were made for an investiture on 16 June 1975 by the governor-general, Jules Léger, at the official residence of the Nova Scotia lieutenant-governor in Halifax. The Dalhousie story repeated itself. 'I went there in absolute terror,' he wrote, 'but everyone (including the Governor-General and particularly, Madame Léger) was so kind to me that, once the beakers of scotch were brought out, I really had a good time.'[20]

Institutional and government recognition were accompanied in the seventies by a wave of academic recognition. This had started in the sixties, and the first major move came from an American university. Early in 1967, Buckler received a letter from Howard Gotlieb, chief of special collections, Boston University, which ended as follows: 'I am sure that many institutions have been in contact with you asking that they might become the repository of your manuscripts and correspondence files. I write to say that Boston University would be honoured to establish an Ernest Buckler collection.'[21] Buckler replied, hinting mysteriously at 'the possible claims of family archivists,' but assuring Gotlieb that, if he decided that his papers should go elsewhere, 'you would be the one most likely to receive them.'[22] Gotlieb replied in a way that must have reassured Buckler about the strength of his appeal: 'if and when you do change your mind, I shall be waiting in the wing. Your work is much admired here and it would be very good indeed to collect you.'[23]

Ernest did not inform me at the time of Gotlieb's tempting proposal, and I cannot recall whether my action two years later was spontaneous or was inspired by hearing of the Boston approach. At any rate, I raised the matter of Buckler's papers with the chief librarian at the University of Toronto, Robert Blackburn, and, in September 1969, he arranged to have his senior colleague, David Esplin, go to Centrelea and negotiate the purchase of Buckler's papers. Ernest thus described the 'deal': 'I found Esplin a hell of a good guy to get along with and we went through all my tureens, firkins where manuscripts were filed. He bought the stuff and bore it away with him and I suppose I should be very happy. But, curiously enough, when it went I felt denuded and defoliated.'[24] The university paid Buckler $10,000 for the papers. In those modestly affluent days for universities, the sum could be paid in cash and not in income tax receipts, which, for Buckler, would have been worthless. Esplin performed a second valuable service during his visit. He assessed Evelyn Garbary's papers, collected during her years with O'Connor – besides O'Connor himself, several of the major Irish literary figures were represented – in which Boston University also showed an interest. Ernest and Evelyn had a modest sum in mind, but Esplin declared emphatically that $20,000 was a rock-bottom price. To their delight, Boston University did not question the assessment.

In the seventies, university academic departments began to discover Buckler. He had numerous invitations from universities all across Canada to read, to lecture, or to come for a period of time as a resident instructor. Acadia, his neighbouring university where Evelyn was now firmly established as a teacher of creative writing and as an expert in all aspects of the stage, was the most persistent wooer. The president, James Beveridge, joined with the head of the English Department, Clarence Tracy, to press home the invitation. But Buckler stoutly resisted what was the most attractive of all the offers – in salary, in responsibilities, in personal convenience – despite the attempts that both Evelyn and I made to dissuade him.

He could not overcome what was now a settled resistance to all change. He was not averse to playing the master tutor when students and academics wrote or came to see him to discuss either his work or their own. He complained half seriously that his house had become a classroom and that he was serving as a full-time tutor without pay. But he enjoyed this tutorial work immensely. His written comments to even the humblest aspiring writer were serious, detailed, uncompromisingly tough, but, if at all possible, encouraging. He was both amused and impressed by scholarly studies of his own work, amused by the insistence on recondite allusions he had never intended, impressed by critical observations that struck him as illuminating. (He often observed that he never knew exactly what he had said until some astute critic explained it to him.) One study that he enjoyed and praised was John Orange's MA dissertation at Toronto, 'Ernest Buckler: The Masks of the Artist' (1970). Orange went on to publish *Ernest Buckler: An Annotated Bibliography* (Toronto: ECW Press, 1981), the indispensable book for any study of him. And Buckler was delighted by William French's long article in the *Globe and Mail* on 24 June 1972 that took up the entire front page of the Entertainment section beneath the page-wide heading 'Ernest Buckler: a literary giant scorned?' The article sketched Buckler's career in a warm and sympathetic manner, ending, however, with a premonitory warning of the 'thin spreading of his talent.'

National awards, honorary degrees, and invitations to teach or lecture were not of great significance to Buckler. For the most part, they were a disturbance, an intrusion on his private life, although his responses were always polite and thoughtful. What did please him was the increasing interest in his work among his fellow Canadian writers, especially those whom he admired.

Many of them wrote to him about his work, and their comments had an apocalyptic quality. They wrote as disciples to the master. Thus, Margaret Laurence: 'We, and I mean writers like me and all the young ones as well, owe you so damn much. You made it all possible. You showed us how to be ourselves. You told us where we really lived.'[25] Alice Munro: 'I have been thinking of you lately, I don't know why. I guess because I've been writing a story called *Home*, which I was thinking you would understand. I don't know if it's similarity of background or vision, but I feel very close to you as a writer.'[26] Marian Engel: 'I don't know where you got the courage, but you have provided generations of writers and readers with joy and self-knowledge, and thank you for it.'[27]

Most of the specific references to Buckler were to *The Mountain and the Valley*. It had come out when a new generation of Canadian writers were beginning to emerge and were looking for direction. Al Purdy (who introduced himself to Buckler in his letter with the tag 'that I write poetry') wrote: 'I read that book 3–4 years ago, and thought then that it was the best novel I had seen by a Canadian. I haven't changed my mind since.'[28] Alistair MacLeod, who, like Buckler, draws deeply on his Nova Scotia background, wrote: '*The Mountain and the Valley* is one of the most powerful and rending novels that I have ever read and I do not think it is because I identify. Somewhere, I think concerning Alden Nowlan, you said something to the effect that the test of good fiction is whether or not we think of it again. Your novel has been on my mind almost too much since my reading it. It somehow will not go away, perhaps that is why I am writing this.'[29]

Spontaneous tributes like this awakened Buckler's interest in Canadian literature. He had never been strongly conscious of writing in a Canadian tradition. Most of his reading had been in English and American fiction. Now, however, he became aware that there was a new literary environment in Canada that had swept aside the old moorings. Consciousness of this change came to him acutely during the two years from 1971 to 1973 when he served on the fiction jury for the Governor-General's Literary Awards. His appointment was another indication of his swelling reputation. He accepted the appointment with alacrity but with some bitter ruminations on the complete disregard the sapient judges had hitherto shown for his work. 'I know damn well,' he wrote to Barbara Hutchinson, 'that an "un-in" type like myself would have little chance in the politics which, I gather, surrounds that plum.'[30]

Buckler took his job as a judge seriously, and supported his judgments trenchantly. He was at his best as a critic when he summarized the particular virtues of a writer. About Mordecai Richler's *St. Urbain's Horseman*, which he placed first for the 1971 award, he wrote: 'Richler has whitstoned his teeth on the hardest bone of all, the bone of truth. He is a born writer, and so sure-footed that one never fears that he'll lose command of his material. Writing seems as natural to him as breathing.' About Margaret Atwood's *Surfacing*, which he placed first for the 1972 award, he wrote: 'Most writers merely skim the surface of life like water-bugs; Atwood dives to the very core.

Surfacing from this book, one meets again the erosion of dailiness but is somehow braced against it by this consummately guided tour through the very nerve endings of meaning and significance. No tricks here. Each sentence is perfect, and Atwood is a poet; but there is here nothing of the ladyish poetastical or even the Mailerish poetesticle.' For both 1971 and 1972 he thought Robertson Davies was a potent contender. Indeed for 1971 he had placed *Fifth Business* first, until it was pointed out that it was published in 1970. About the 1972 award he wrote to me:

If there were any question of another book's overtaking *Surfacing*, or even passing it, it would be the *Manticore*. I've always had reservations about Davies. Too cerebral? Too damned 'knowing' about how much he knows? His impeccable sentences too damned enamelled? In this book (though I wish he wouldn't still keep using those Sheridanish names (Unworthy, McQuilly, Miss Gostling), there is something new: a heartbeat. He still writes with nearly forbidding wit and dismaying exactitude, and every page is studded with perception and apperception – but it's this new 'humanity' if you like, that adds immeasurably to the book's stature. Besides that, *Manticore* is a corking good story on all accounts and when has readability, though often snippily scorned, ever been a real demerit?[31]

During the two years Buckler served on the fiction committee, Margaret Laurence did not publish a novel. If she had, there would have been no doubt about his first choice. He looked upon Margaret Laurence as the 'big one' in Canadian literature. Although they never met, she was, among contemporary Canadian writers, the one closest to him. In the summer of 1974, she sent him through friends a copy of *The Diviners*, with a warm inscription. He found it 'a fine, powerful and deeply moving book. Solid as steel (though never for an instant steely), and searching as only the great heart is equipped to be.'[32] They corresponded at regular intervals during the next four years. Buckler was overjoyed when she wrote a flattering review of his book of short stories, a book that he had not initiated and about which he was apprehensive. She elaborated on her appraisal in a letter to him.

I'd never read any of your stories before, and it was like discovering buried treasure or something. Wow! They are so good, Ernie. So many things fascinated me about them – the ways in which some of them adumbrated themes in *The Mountain and the Valley* and *The Cruelest Month* (or so it seemed to me); the way in which you can control the exact tone of the human voice, with a use of idiom that is never overdone or caricatured, so that the reader has the feeling of actually hearing people speaking; the way in which the stories communicate the sense of place so beautifully, so that the reader is enabled for a while to enter, really to enter, your country, your place. Another thing – the way in which you can communicate and make comprehensible the sadness and even tragedy of those hurtful silences between people who love each other, and the subtleties of father-son and brother-brother relationships, in which each must tread very carefully, but never, it seems, can tread quite carefully enough.[33]

In his reply Buckler silenced his own doubts, and accepted her praise 'because you recognize precisely what I was (at least) trying to do and precisely what my goals (at least) were. I could never write you: you're too big; but you could write me, better than I can. So "in the company of angels and archangels" I bless you.'[34]

When the Writers' Union elected him as its first honorary member in October 1974, Buckler was pleased; he was deeply moved when he heard later from Margaret Laurence about the sponsorship of the election motion and what it said. 'Peggy Atwood made the motion,' she wrote, 'and I seconded it; and we both talked a bit about you and how much we all owed you, and I did say to the younger writers, "You're not writing out of colonial models any more, and the reason you aren't is because people like Buckler learned, by themselves, how to write out of what is truly ours, and you had better not forget how much you owe him." '[35]

CHAPTER SEVEN

Last Years

Without leaving Centrelea (except for a few short trips dictated by circumstances), Buckler had become in the seventies a minor public figure – a critic whose judgments were respected, a man of letters honoured by universities and the nation, and a confidant of writers, both established and aspiring. A result of this new status was a great expansion in Buckler's correspondence. This he welcomed. He had always been a faithful letter-writer, letters were part of his literary life, to be composed with care, within a general framework of informality. In the seventies he continued his regular correspondence with Margaret Bickley Farmer and to me, but now a number of other correspondents to whom he wrote faithfully. Most of them were fellow writers. Chief of them was Margaret Laurence, who gave him the discriminating praise that he needed and loved, and to whom he wrote with candour about his problems of body and mind. (He never met Margaret Laurence, a visit that she had planned had to be abandoned.) He never met three other writers with whom he corresponded at this time. Manuel Komroff, prolific writer and influential editor, and Arnold Gingrich, who had returned to *Esquire* as editor in 1952 after an absence of seven years, resumed their correspondence with the brilliant young star of the 'The Sound and the Fury' column of the thirties, and Buckler was delighted to bring them up to date on his literary career. A new correspondent was Harold Brown, an American novelist living in Mexico whose books, *A Walk in the Sun, The Cos-*

tumed Soldier, The Wild Hunt, Stars in Their Courses, A Quiet Place to Work, had drawn critical attention and aroused considerable popular appeal (two of them had been made into movies).

Brown had published through Knopf, and Angus Cameron, Buckler's editor for *Ox Bells and Fireflies,* had asked Brown for a promotional comment. Brown had responded with great enthusiasm, and subsequently wrote to Buckler: 'I'm now sorry that I forgot to say that it's a book I intend to read once every year for the 32 years that remain to me (I intend to be around on New Year's day, 2001, if only to be able to spit on the 21st Century).'[1] In subsequent correspondence, Brown wrote of the great literary world of which he was occasionally a part – stories of Norman Mailer, and of a cocktail party given by Cyril Connolly in the spring of 1944 in London where the guests of honour were Hemingway and Koestler. (At the time, Brown was in the American army, and attached to the office of War Information in London.) Brown sent Buckler a number of his novels, and Buckler replied a little in the style of the apprentice saluting the master. Brown did not accept the implied judgment. When Buckler wrote to him about the sale of his papers to the University of Toronto, he replied: 'I was pleased as punch that the U. of T. has given tangible proof that you are (a) a better writer than I, and (b) more highly regarded in Groves of Academe. I love them all – lock, stock, and Bissell (with the librarian thrown in).'[2]

Other correspondents of the seventies were friends he saw from time to time. The actor Arthur Kennedy and his wife kept in touch during their long absence from their house near Annapolis Royal and even after they left it for good. Kennedy would telephone from various distant places, often about a literary scheme in which he thought Buckler might be interested. (He never was.) When Buckler went to the Lahey Clinic in Boston, Kennedy arranged for him to see the current play in which he was appearing (a minor effort that never reached Broadway). Like Brown, the Kennedys were Ernest's link to the great world that he viewed with wonder and delight but with no desire to experience at first hand. To the Kennedys he wrote long letters brimming with affection and admiration, punctuated with a bawdy limerick or an acidulous comment on a local worthy. New friends were Joan and Al McGuire, from southern Ontario, introduced to him by Rachel Grover, a University of Toronto librarian in the Department of Rare Books and Special Collections, who greatly admired Buckler's work and had eagerly assumed the responsibility for the organization of his papers. The McGuires were book lovers and Buckler admirers also; they and Rachel Grover visited him several times during the mid-seventies, bringing presents of books, records (including an autographed record of Ernest's great favourite, Leontyne Price), and exotic food. Ernest looked forward to their visits. In a letter to all three, he expressed his delight with genially comic exaggeration:

You know, of course, that you've ruined my career. I can never go back to celebrate the peasant (which has been my stock in trade heretofore) as the exclusive salt of the earth. Not since you 'city-people' have shown me how some of you can be so much more big-and-capacious-hearted, so much less mean-spirited, so much more restoratively understanding of each other's troubles, so much more generous in instinctively generous offers to help a troubled guy.[3]

Two other Canadian correspondents were 'Silver Donald' Cameron and Hans Weber, both, in varying degrees, professional associates. Cameron had left academic life in the Maritimes to become a full-time writer, and he found a sympathetic adviser and friend in Buckler. He sent Buckler his published work, a biographical study of Leacock, for instance, and consulted him about his fiction. He taped an interview with Buckler that he published in a literary periodical he edited. It was revealingly entitled, 'A conversation with an Irritated Oyster.' Hans Weber was, as we already know, Buckler's collaborator in *Window on the Sea*. Ernest accompanied him on his photographic excursions through the countryside of Nova Scotia, and a close attachment grew between the two – the aging writer

(Ernest was now in his mid-sixties), conscious of the years closing in on him, and the young man in his early twenties, talented and free of daily worries, confident of the future. Ernest's letters are warm and affectionate, full of details about his daily life.

Throughout his literary career Buckler had a good deal of correspondence with agents and editors. He was always mild and conciliatory even when faced with bluntly worded rejections. But with some editors (particularly with two from McClelland and Stewart, Jack Rackliffe of *The Cruelest Month* and Pamela Fry of *Window on the Sea*), the relationship was close to master and disciple. The only publisher with whom he corresponded was Jack McClelland, an association strengthened by a genial and vinous meeting in 1973. McClelland was a firm supporter of *Ox Bells and Fireflies*. He wrote, 'it gave me more pleasure, more enjoyment, more emotional involvement than anything that has come my way in a very long time.'4 But in the mid-seventies the correspondence was about *Whirligig* about which McClelland and his editors had grave doubts. Indeed, its publication was delayed for several years until Buckler produced additional material. His final letter to McClelland (14 April 1977) was the last letter he wrote on professional matters. It was an expression of pleasure at the decision to go ahead with *Whirligig*, with a typically wry twist: he was confident that, since his mother's maiden name was Swift, he could get along well with his new editor, Diana Swift, 'on the grounds of consanguinity.'

The increase in Ernest's correspondence was, in part, a result of his growing eminence. But it was also a defence against the swift disintegration of his private life, never at any time a perdurable structure. The seventies began with the collapse of his close relation with Evelyn Garbary, about whom he had written to friends, in the first years after their meeting, with the ardour of a lover. There was no specific incident that brought about the estrangement, but the general causes are not hard to seek. Ernest could be unreasonably demanding, and Evelyn was more and more immersed in her responsibilities at Acadia, which often took her away for lengthy periods. He had a wandering, although usually innocent, eye for women – young students or middle-aged admirers – who came to visit the author of *The Mountain and the Valley*. (When, in August 1987, we went to see Evelyn Garbary, retired and living in an old house in Wolfville that was full of books and pictures that mirrored her crowded past, she spoke of Ernest with affection and admiration.)

There was a steady decline in his health during the seventies. Letters, formerly full of speculations about his writing and laced with quotations from his current book in progress, now gave first place to lengthy bulletins about his health (although, even at their darkest, relieved with touches of humour); the headache that had been his persistent affliction since youth now had a pervasive intensity. 'The head is getting worse all the time – the ache used to be steady but sort of organized; now it is violently anarchic.'[5] The headache was never diagnosed (except for the suggestion that it had psychological roots). Even the elaborate check-up at the Lahey Clinic turned up only a small growth on the bowel (fortunately benign), which was removed with little after-effect, either good or bad. Subsequent tests in Halifax reached a more elaborate and diverse diagnosis: he suffered from polythemia (an excess of blood vessels in the head), diverticulitis, and hypertension. Unfortunately the only treatment seemed to be the taking of a variety of pills. 'I'm stuffed,' he proclaimed to Margaret, 'with hypertension pills, sleeping draughts, something called "muscle relaxants" etc. and consequently my head feels like a total cinder.'[6] Whatever the precise nature of his afflictions, the reality was terrifying: 'I'm literally at wit's end. Waking up each day to the dismay of however I can get through the hours before sleep (sleep? Ha Ha Now there's the most accomplished Gethsemane: Insomnia). Then wandering through simple darkness like a sleep walker. Wondering from moment to moment how I can hold up from moment to moment, longing almost for collapse ... but having not to.'[7]

Towards the end of the decade, there was a series of events of a profoundly disturbing nature that accelerated Buckler's decline. Suddenly, as he wrote to Margaret Laurence, it was 'as if death was a contagious disease.' In 1975 and 1976, his two old American mentors, now vivid in his mind from a revived correspondence, Manuel Komroff and Arnold Gingrich, died, as did Mary Kennedy, Arthur Kennedy's wife, to whom he was deeply attached. An even more disturbing death was that of Roy Laurence. From his home in Annapolis, Laurence and his wife Mona had been regular and eagerly awaited visitors, and Roy had arranged the Lahey trip and accompanied Ernest on it. Ernest wrote to me about the funeral:

The funeral was very unorthodox. He had stipulated (with levity I'm sure, because I doubt that he's ever really thought about dying) that he didn't want a church ceremony when he died, but just a festive outdoor gathering of friends. That's how it was done. A sort of garden party, with bar attached – on the beautiful lawn behind his lovely house. In a curious way – it wasn't robust enough to be a wake – it was almost more macabre than the orthodox alternative; and poor Mona, his wife, had to keep on a face-for-the occasion for three killing hours.[8]

This succession of deaths was of friends who were close to Ernest in age (in 1976 he was sixty-eight) – most of them his senior by a few years. Then in 1978 came the sudden death by accident of Hans Weber, still in his twenties. Ernest wrote to me about the tragedy. It was hand-written, the individual letters shakily formed, and the lines now crowded together, now wandering uncertainly – a cry from the heart.

Now, I've had shattering news. Dear Hans has just been killed. No one knows what happened. He was alone in the car. The news has literally devastated me. The doctor wants me in hospital, but there are so many reasons why I can't assent – my feelings are so knocked about and battered that I can't decide anything. Hans was such a friend and more.

I'm sorry to sadden you with this news, but I can't help it. Everything cries out 'Hans is dead!' I can't write any more ... I'm stricken.

How long does heart-brokenness last? I hope I never have to go through days like this, but I suppose in time I'll heal.[9]

Death had been a frequent subject in Buckler's fiction – dealt with unsentimentally but movingly as a sudden arrest in time, a kind of utter silence when objects seemed to retire within themselves. In his last formal piece of writing, he made death his subject, and, as he commented, wrote it, 'with his heart's blood.' The piece was called 'The Orchard' and it appeared in the *Imperial Oil Review* in 1979. It was written the previous year. It is an autobiographical recollection of a sister, who was born and died before he was born. For the young boy who is the narrator, his sister's death means a few keepsakes – a tiny cardboard cross, a small, beaded change-purse, a tiny braid of golden hair – but it is also 'a quality in the air that I had never noticed before. Quieter than silence. Quieter than mysteries. Death is "distance," the cruelest word in the language; something that strips things of their power to merge with other things, and isolates man from the world around him.'

The piece was a farewell not only to the sister whom he had never known, but to the dear friends who had recently left him. By 1978 it was increasingly clear that he could not stay in the house by himself. Besides his rapidly declining health, there was the impossible burden now placed upon his two sisters, who had hitherto kept an eye on him and made sure that there was sufficient food in the house (and food when he had visitors on a generous and succulent scale). In 1976 Nelly and her husband Harold finally confronted the fact that they must leave the old homestead in West Dalhousie and go to the retirement home in Bridgetown. Ernest left his own house and stayed with his sister and brother-in-law while they prepared for departure. This was the house of Ernest's childhood, the house to which he had returned after his years in Toronto and where he had begun his career as a writer. 'My sister and her husband,' he wrote to Margaret Laurence, 'have finally moved from house to Home. The packing left us almost snow-bound from the blizzard of memory.'[10] Ernest was also distressed about the move to the retirement home. He was, in many ways, a prisoner of the past, and he thought of the home as 'the poor house,' the ultimate humiliation that threatened everybody. He slowly absorbed the fact that 'Mountain Lea' was not a 'poor house.' It was subsidized for the indigent, but others paid in accordance with their resources; and he was a little proud of the fact that Nelly and Harold would be paying a substantial monthly charge. But, conscious that a similar fate awaited him, he talked darkly about Mountain Lea as the 'Loneliness Hilton,' with 'immaculate corridors like death rows.'

Ernest moved into Mountain Lea in 1981. In the summer of 1980 there had been an unhappy prologue to the move. Dr Mahaney had sent him to Halifax for another check-up (he had been hallucinating and was unable to use the typewriter, which had been essential to him for an orderly and happy existence). But, unknown to Ernest, he had been sent to the hospital at Dartmouth, which, given his symptoms, was a logical choice. But this disturbed Ernest. Just as the retirement home was the poor house of his youth, so the Dartmouth hospital was, in the folklore of Nova Scotia, the place where the feeble-minded went. He wrote to me from Dartmouth. 'I've been very much confined these last months (the request for a cigarette has to be notarized). But if I do get sprung, you'll hear from me in the near future.'[11] When we went to see Ernest in September, he was living with Olive and Ray, and all three were waiting for vacancies at Mountain Lea. Ernest had now recovered from his Dartmouth ordeal. He spoke about it, however, with some bitterness. He resented being sent there, where old men sat in the halls impassively, spitting on the floor, or shouting incoherently. When, on his first night, he put on his dressing gown, his roommate told him angrily 'to take that thing off of you.' But he was now sufficiently removed from the hospital to speak of it with his old ironic humour. He recalled the psychiatrist, a little, unimpressive man who began each sentence with 'Now, about those dreams?' followed by a little nervous cough. Ernest was unresponsive; he had had no dreams. The psychiatrist then lost interest in him, and they talked about the recent death of the Shah of Iran. Ernest was soon released from the usual routine, and dined out in the town, on one occasion at the home of the chief administrator, who was a friend of Evelyn Garbary.

Mountain Lea is a single-storey building on the northern edge of Bridgetown, pleasantly extended, with unimpeded views of broad fields and the north mountains of the valley. It has a refreshingly unbureaucratic atmosphere, and the staff give the impression that they are not working under pressure or duress. We came there first in September 1981. We found Ernest's room quickly. He was sitting on his chair, and rose with delight to greet us. The room was a narrow cubicle with only enough space for a single bed, a dresser, and a chair. On the wall above his head, he had hung a collage that Christine had made and brought to him when he was still in his house. It was an evocation of *The Mountain and the Valley* and *Window on the Sea* fashioned from Cape Breton materials.

There were a few books piled on the dresser, a card from the governor-general, and a photograph that I had sent him some time ago. Later on, his old upright typewriter was brought over from the house, but he could never use it.

Ernest was beginning to take on some of the characteristics of old age; he was a little bent, and his face had assumed an air of gentle resignation. The voice was low and often faint, as if articulation were too much of a strain. But he was still adept on his feet, negotiating stairs with assurance. And compared to most of his fellow residents, he looked and acted like an active soldier among the walking wounded.

On this visit and in three later visits, we took Ernest for a drive and had a meal at a restaurant, where he would eat with gusto unknown in his Centrelea days. Conversation while driving was difficult, since he could be heard only with difficulty above the sound of the engine. But when we stopped to look at something of interest, the old wit would emerge. The 'survival humour' that had carried him through the bitter years of the seventies was still operative. I recall a few examples. We had stopped at an antique shop that specialized in old farm tools. I examined a large axe that would have delighted an Elizabethan executioner. The blade had been sunk lightly in a block of wood. I plied the blade free to examine it more carefully, then found that I could not easily imbed it again in the wood. Ernest seized the handle, and with a sharp motion buried the blade deeply. I expressed surprise and admiration. He smiled. 'I practise daily with Excalibur,' he said. On another trip, in May when it was still cold and windy, we went to the old house at Centrelea. Nothing was changed. Ernest walked through apparently unmoved, although his mind must have been 'a blizzard of memories.' In the parlour I stopped to look at the gloomy picture on the wall, in which a black gondola-like boat was labouring against the elements. Ernest glanced outside where the trees were swaying in a strong wind, then followed my gaze to the picture. 'It's bad weather there too,' he said.

For some time I had been thinking of a way to commemorate Ernest's work. His career as a writer had come to an end, and there was certainly a strong possibility that he would not be with us for long. I thought of the deserted house at Centrelea as a museum, as Ernest would have said, of itself. Could it be purchased and turned into a museum devoted to Buckler's work and perhaps to the work of other Maritime writers? I wrote letters to the Nova Scotia minister of education and the chairman of the Canada Council, but, as I had anticipated, got polite replies of rejection. The financial problem was too great for the province, and the Canada Council had ruled out projects of such a nature. I turned to a more modest idea – a seminar on Buckler in his home town, with an attendant celebration. Then after some communications with my friend, Roy McIsaac, then the mayor of Bridgetown, I concluded that a modest local gathering would be best, with tributes to Buckler and a presentation. Even this idea would, I thought, be difficult to implement. Buckler was not clearly a Bridgetown boy. He had spent his life near Bridgetown, not in it, and I could detect in him no strong attachment to the town. What about Buckler himself? He disliked crowds, quaked at the thought of making a public speech. Roy McIsaac convinced me, however, that the idea of a local affair was sound: he knew that a faithful band of Buckler's friends and admirers existed and there was no need for Ernest to give a speech.

The night before the event, which was to take place on Saturday, 11 September 1982, we drove down from Cape Breton and arrived at Bridgetown in late afternoon. We went over early in the evening to Mountain Lea, where the Buckler tribute was to take place, and, to our delight, discovered a relaxed and benign Ernest. He was, his sisters said, looking forward to the event, and had even consented to go with them to town to buy a new suit – light grey, instead of the dark blue prescribed for weddings, funerals, and ceremonial occasions. When we left a little after nine, Ernest was welcoming a young nurse. 'It was nice,' he observed. 'to have geisha girls put you to bed.'

On Saturday, we came to Mountain Lea at 1:00 p.m., an hour before the gathering was to begin. In the assembly room, where we were to meet, all was in readiness. A long table was already laden with cheese, biscuits, fruit, and wine (local) was in the offing. Nearby on a small table were displayed Ernest's books, his medals (the Order of Canada, the centennial medal, the Leacock Medal for Humour, and two medals for short-story competitions), and his three honorary degree hoods. Guests began to arrive, and soon the room was crowded. To my alarm, the wine was brought in immediately, the guests moved in on the cheese and fruit, and little animated groups began to form. I knew from experience that such a gathering is fiercely resistant to speeches, and I wondered how the chairman, the mayor, could convert these happy chatting groups into a silent and receptive audience. There was no platform to confer authority on the chairman, and it took him some time to gain attention. Finally the last group fell silent and the speeches began.

The mayor was brief, not extending his 'words' much beyond an introduction of me. I made some personal remarks, read passages from Buckler's books, and presented the tributes we had received from Margaret Laurence, Margaret Atwood, William French, Max Ferguson, and Jack McClelland, and then called upon Nelly and Olive to unveil the picture of Ernest that had been prepared for the occasion. Actually it was a photograph enlarged to the size of an average oil portrait and framed conventionally. The only picture available was Ernest's graduating picture at Dalhousie, not, I thought, the most appropriate for the occasion. But it was, in its way, impressive – a portrait of the artist as a young man, the solemn features and concentrated gaze masking the inner life.

During the speeches and the unveiling Ernest sat at a table to the left of the speakers with Nelly (Olive had somehow got separated and was in the main body). After the unveiling he arose twice, a piece of paper in his hand. Each time the mayor motioned him to take his seat. Then finally at the moment he thought appropriate, he invited Ernest to speak. Ernest rose, a slight, almost apologetic figure, rapidly read one formal sentence of thanks, and sat down visibly relieved.

The speeches continued. Greg Cook, a former Acadia lecturer and a student of Buckler's work, introduced Mrs Kaye Hill, an executive in the Nova Scotia Writers' Union. She told how as a young girl she had walked up and down in front of Ernest's house, not bold enough to knock on the door. Now, she had an opportunity to take advantage of him, and proposed to kiss him (which she proceeded to do). Bill Percy, a novelist who lived a few miles away, brought official presidential greetings from the writers' union. (After Ernest's death he wrote a beautiful sensitive tribute to him: 'Sleight of Heart,' in *Books in Canada*, May 1984.) Miss Montgomery, the head of the nursing service at Mountain Lea, then read a letter from Bill Howell, a CBC producer and poet, who had become a writer through Ernest's encouragement. Finally the chairman called upon a few dignitaries (the audience included the MP and the MPP from the area, and the clergymen of the three main churches) to give their blessings.

The audience, released from oratorical bondage, broke up again into informal groups. Jerry Orlando, a handsome widow and an old friend of Ernest, took her place at the piano and played popular dance songs with a strong, insistent rhythm. A jolly middle-aged lady, Ernest's cousin Opal, danced out to the centre in time to the music, and the mayor joined her. Then suddenly Ernest was on his feet and was dancing in a spirited way with Nelly. The audience was delighted and applauded. (Ernest later said that he was sorry Christine and he had no chance to do their Ginger Rogers–Fred Astaire act.) The audience now began to drift outside to the lawn. The day was warm and brilliantly sunny, and the mood was friendly and relaxed. Ernest stood near the door, talking to old friends and relatives.

At 6:30 p.m. we gave a dinner party at the local inn for Ernest, Nelly, Olive and Raymond, the McIsaacs and Mahaneys. We returned to Mountain Lea, where Ernest was his old self, describing with animation books he had just read – Muggeridge's autobiography, Updike's *Rabbit Is Rich* – recalling his delight many years ago in James Agee's *A Death in the Family*. We left at 9:30 p.m., long after all the other residents of Mountain Lea had retired.

The Mahaneys invited us back for a night-cap. At midnight we suddenly realized that the new day was our wedding anniversary. The Mahaneys insisted that we should stay on to celebrate. At 2:00 a.m. when we left, the night was still balmy and warm and the little town was silent and deserted. We thought of Ernest, whom we had left in his narrow room, and how he would have enjoyed these unconvenanted hours of drink and talk.

Our last visit took place in August 1983. In the meantime Olive's husband, the genial, relaxed Raymond, after an operation for cancer, and Nelly's husband Harold, at the age of ninety, had both died. The two sisters now occupied a room together across the hall from Ernest. The room was filled with family pictures and keepsakes and, conspicuously, with a row of first editions of all of Ernest's books that Nelly had proudly assembled over the years. Ernest was half-lying, half-sitting in a chair, nattily dressed in a blue pullover, blue trousers, and blue slippers – a bold departure for him in style and colour, undoubtedly the work of his devoted sisters. He had not been well. He had

had a bowel infection, which had been serious and relentless and had reduced him to child-like dependence. The condition had improved but he had been left with painful haemorrhoids, which as he inched himself up slowly in his seat he observed 'must be only less agonizing than childbirth.'

In his room there were some signs of literary activity – a few official letters neatly arranged (royalty statements chiefly – the sales of *The Mountain and the Valley* still surged ahead), some books, my first volume of the Massey biography, which I had sent him and about which he wrote a perceptive letter, and a copy of Mathew's biography of Frank O'Connor, which contained many references to Evelyn Garbary. He showed his usual keen interest in members of our family, and was delighted by Christine's story of our grandson Alexander, aged four. Alexander had had an unhappy day at a summer school he was attending, and had reported: 'I cried a lot, but not as much as a horse.' Ernest was delighted by the use of the word 'horse.' 'No other word – "cow", for instance – would have done,' Ernest declared.

When the time came to leave, Ernest seemed relaxed, with no suggestion of the emotional upset that usually marked departures. But Olive and Nelly, when we saw them together in their room, were tearful. 'You don't think he's going soon?' asked Nelly, and I sincerely replied, 'No.'

I was wrong. The reports from Mountain Lea over the next few months became more and more disturbing. Around the turn of the year Nelly reported that Ernest was passive and withdrawn. In late February he had been sent to the hospital with a severe case of pneumonia and had shown no signs of recognition when Olive and Nelly visited him. He died on 4 March 1984. We were unable to attend the funeral. My brother Lester who had been in hospital for over a year died on 8 March.

Ernest was buried in the cemetery beside the little Anglican church that had for decades served the West Dalhousie community. It was a holy place for him. A few years before his death we had visited the cemetery, and he had said with deep emotion: 'This is the place I love best. This is where I could come every day.' Here death lost its icy distance and menacing silence.

Their dead had been dead so long that all the challenge had been sifted out of their silence. And the grave-statement here merely gentled the air, engraved it (and you) with such contentment it was like an unseen fleece cushioning the edges of the breeze.[12]

Notes

CHAPTER ONE: LIFE WITH ERNEST

1 E. Buckler to C.T. Bissell, 16 December 1960
2 'Fiction' in 'Letters in Canada, 1953,' *University of Toronto Quarterly*, 1 April 1953, 290–1
3 Buckler to Bissell, n.d. (probably August 1953)
4 Journal, 28 December 1935
5 Adapted from a passage in *Ox Bells and Fireflies*, 45
6 Buckler to Pierre Berton, 4 April 1951
7 Buckler to Bissell, 1 January 1954
8 Buckler to Bissell, 1 January 1954
9 Buckler to Bissell, 7 July 1954
10 Buckler to Bissell, 28 June 1955
11 *The Cruelest Month*, 259
12 *Ox Bells and Fireflies*, 167
13 Ibid., 188
14 Buckler to Bill Howell, 4 November 1969
15 Buckler to Bissell, 22 December 1972
16 *Ox Bells and Fireflies*, 190
17 Ibid., 188
18 Buckler to Bissell, 4 June 1960
19 From an unidentified manuscript, in all likelihood one of his articles in *Saturday Night*, which appeared between June 1947 and November 1948.

20 Changed to 'Last Stop before Paradise' in *Maclean's*, 1 June 1949, 22–3.
21 *The Mountain and the Valley*, 200
22 Ibid., 89
23 Ibid., 90
24 Buckler to Mary and John Kennedy, undated
25 Buckler to Mary and John Kennedy, 13 March 1972
26 Buckler to Bissell, 19 May 1964
27 Buckler to Bissell, 3 February 1959

CHAPTER TWO: APPRENTICESHIP

1 Buckler to Bissell, 16 December 1960
2 *Ox Bells and Fireflies*, 71
3 'The Clumsy One,' in *The Rebellion of Young David*, 54
4 *Family Herald*, 24 April 1958
5 *The Mountain and the Valley*, 14
6 Buckler to Harry Brown, 1 April 1969
7 Mrs Faren to Buckler, 19 July 1935
8 From two letters of recommendation, 6 April and 8 April 1935
9 This was written in 1928, and is quoted in a letter written by a young Bridgetown girl with whom Ernest had a high-minded love affair. I am grateful to Mrs Orlando of Bridgetown who let me see the letter.
10 Buckler to Bissell, 16 December 1961
11 Buckler to Ted Bentley, 9 September 1937
12 Journal, 3 March 1936
13 'The Sound and the Fury,' *Esquire*, January 1939
14 This is from a manuscript that was presumably to be incorporated in a 'Maritime Letter' in *Saturday Night*.
15 'The Best Place to Be,' in *Whirligig*, 11–12
16 Journal, 15 June 1936
17 Buckler to Al and Joan McGuire, 10 July 1977
18 Journal, 18 December 1936
19 Buckler to Bissell, 8 September 1969
20 *The Trinity University Review*, 46 (December 1933), 74–6
21 Journal, 3 December 1935

22 Andrew Clark to Buckler, 16 February 1969
23 Journal, 18–19 October 1936
24 Ibid.
25 Buckler to Alexander Woollcott, undated
26 'The Sound and the Fury,' *Esquire* (March 1977)
27 Ibid.
28 Ibid. (May 1937)
29 A. Gingrich, *Nothing But People: The Early Days at* Esquire, *a Personal History, 1929–1958* (New York: Crowe Publishers 1971), 253
30 Ted Bentley to Buckler, 26 July 1937
31 Manuel Komroff to Buckler, 29 December 1939
32 Komroff to Buckler, 12 June 1939
33 Komroff to Buckler, 23 October 1938
34 Gingrich, *Nothing But People,* 253
35 Burton Rascoe to Buckler, n.d. (probably March 1937)
36 Journal, 17 December 1936
37 Ibid., 8 January 1936
38 Ibid., 16 March 1937
39 'The Sound and the Fury,' *Esquire* (June 1938)
40 Ibid. (May 1937)
41 Ibid. (March 1937)
42 Buckler to Arnold Gingrich, 21 June 1939

CHAPTER THREE: PROMISES FULFILLED

1 Buckler to John Bennett, assistant editor of *Esquire,* 28 May 1952
2 B.K. Sandwell to Buckler, 18 November 1940
3 Sandwell to Buckler, 11 December 1941
4 Sandwell to Buckler, 27 September 1943
5 This is from a manuscript that was presumably to be incorporated in a Maritime letter in *Saturday Night.*
6 Buckler to Bissell, 25 April 1975
7 W.O. Mitchell to Buckler, 19 July 1948
8 Buckler to Miss Burton, 25 February 1950
9 Edward Weeks to Buckler, 1 April 1951

10 Reader's report, 25 April 1951
11 Reader's report by Jonathan Loff, 4 March 1952
12 Buckler to Burton Rascoe, 2 March 1937
13 Buckler to William Raney, 14 January 1952
14 *The Mountain and the Valley*, 19
15 Ibid., 229
16 Ibid., 254
17 Ibid., 71
18 Ibid., 74
19 Ibid., 287
20 Ibid., 90
21 Ibid., 52
22 Ibid., 260
23 This is from Buckler's answer to a series of questions posed to him by the publisher of *The Mountain and the Valley*, Henry Holt.
24 *The Mountain and the Valley*, 244
25 Buckler to Albert Knopf, 15 July 1953
26 Buckler to Bissell, 16 December 1960
27 Elizabeth Bowen, *The Last September* (London: Penguin Books 1942), 67
28 *The Mountain and the Valley*, 53
29 Ibid., 121
30 Ibid., 163
31 Buckler to Charles Smith, 22 May 1972
32 *The Mountain and the Valley*, 264–5
33 Sinclair Ross to Buckler, 3 September 1976
34 *The Mountain and the Valley*, 201
35 Buckler to Dudley H. Cloud, 15 May 1951
36 *The Mountain and the Valley*, 289
37 This is from supplementary answers to a questionnaire sent to Buckler by Alfred Knopf, preliminary to the publication of *Ox Bells and Fireflies* in 1968.
38 Buckler to A. Gingrich, 27 January 1953

CHAPTER FOUR: CHARTING THE WASTE LAND

1 *The Cruelest Month*, 41

2 Buckler to Margaret Bickley, 18 December 1953
3 Buckler to Bickley 1958, undated
4 Buckler to Bickley, 28 December 1958
5 *The Cruelest Month*, 68–9
6 Buckler to Bickley, undated (probably early 1959)
7 Buckler to Bickley, 11 August 1959
8 *The Cruelest Month*, 247
9 Ibid., 259
10 Buckler to Bickley 20 April 1961
11 Buckler to Bickley, 28 December 1959
12 *The Cruelest Month*, 16
13 Bickley to Buckler, 8 November 1971
14 Bickley to Buckler, 25 August 1960
15 Buckler to Bickley, 30 December 1956
16 Bickley to Buckler, 18 June 1966
17 Buckler to John and Mary Kennedy, 4 January 1972
18 Buckler to Margaret Bickley Farmer, 17 August 1971
19 *The Cruelest Month*, 74
20 Bickley to Buckler, 22 February 1957
21 Buckler to Bickley, undated (probably late 1959)
22 Buckler to Bickley, 25 November 1958
23 Buckler to Bickley, 16 December 1960
24 Buckler to Bissell, 2 January 1965
25 Buckler to Bickley, 5 May 1958
26 Robert Lescher to Ivan Van Auw Jr., 4 January 1961
27 Bickley to Bissell, 19 December 1959
28 Buckler to Bickley, 27 January 1960
29 Buckler to Bissell, 28 January 1960
30 John Rackliffe to Buckler, 27 September 1961
31 Buckler to Ivan Van Auw Jr., 21 January 1952
32 Buckler to William Raney, 3 September 1952
33 *The Cruelest Month*, 9
34 Ibid., 14
35 Ibid., 14
36 Ibid., 20
37 Ibid., 161
38 Ibid., 89
39 Ibid., 109

40 Buckler to John Rackliffe, 14 October 1961
41 Buckler to Bissell, 21 December 1973
42 *The Cruelest Month*, 62
43 Ibid., 183
44 Buckler to Bissell, 4 June 1960
45 *The Cruelest Month*, 264
46 Ibid., 264–5
47 Ibid., 266
48 Ibid., 276
49 ibid., 276
50 Ibid., 268–9
51 Buckler to Bickley, undated (probably March 1959)
52 Buckler to Bissell, 23 September 1960
53 Buckler to Ivan Van Auw, October 1959
54 Bissell to Buckler, 12 November 1963
55 Buckler to Bissell, 20 November 1963
56 *The Cruelest Month*, 185–6
57 Ibid., 139
58 Buckler to Bissell, 21 December 1973

CHAPTER FIVE: RETURN TO PARADISE

1 Buckler to Ivan Van Auw, 21 January 1952
2 'The Best Place to Be,' in *Whirligig*, 10
3 An open letter to the CBC, 29 April 1965
4 Leonard Brockington to Buckler, 20 June 1944
5 Brockington to Buckler, 20 September 1964
6 Buckler to Brockington, 25 September 1964
7 Buckler to Evelyn Garbary, 6 February 1966
8 Buckler to Christine Bissell, 12 October 1964
9 Buckler to Bissell, 10 May 1965
10 Buckler to Garbary, 29 April 1965
11 Garbary to Buckler, 27 April 1965
12 Buckler to Garbary, 30 April 1965
13 Garbary to Bissell, undated (probably March 1988)
14 Garbary to Buckler, 11 November 1965
15 Angus Cameron to Buckler, 31 January 1968

16 Barbara Burgess to Buckler, 4 April 1978
17 Buckler to William Raney, 3 September 1952
18 Buckler to Ivan Van Auw, undated (probably 1953)
19 *Ox Bells and Fireflies*, 133
20 Ibid., 20
21 Ibid., 130–1
22 Ibid., 6
23 Ibid., 17–18
24 Ibid., 302
25 Ibid., 103
26 ibid., 219
27 Ibid., 247
28 Ibid., 85
29 Bissell to Buckler, 27 August 1965
30 Buckler to Bissell, 30 August 1965
31 *Ox Bells and Fireflies*, 6
32 Ibid., 21
33 This was Buckler's explanation of his method and intention in an answer to his publisher's questionnaire.

CHAPTER SIX: MAN OF LETTERS

1 Buckler to Bickley, 11 June 1969
2 Buckler to Bissell, 29 March 1970
3 *Nova Scotia: Window on the Sea*, 12
4 Ibid., 12
5 Ibid., 16
6 Ibid., 96
7 Buckler to Pamela Fry, 19 January 1971
8 *Window on the Sea*, 109
9 Ibid., 12
10 Ibid., 112
11 Ibid., 27
12 Ibid., 125
13 Margaret Laurence to Buckler, 15 December 1974
14 Buckler to Christine and Claude Bissell, 7 December 1970
15 Buckler to Bissell, 4 January 1972

16 Buckler to Bissell, 15 November 1973
17 Buckler to Bissell, 11 March 1968
18 *Window on the Sea*, 14–15
19 Buckler to Bickley, 16 March 1971
20 Buckler to Bickley, 26 June 1975
21 H. Gotlieb to Buckler, 3 January 1967
22 Buckler to Gotlieb, 18 January 1967
23 Gotlieb to Buckler, 14 January 1967
24 Buckler to Bickley, 10 September 1969
25 Margaret Laurence to Buckler, 13 November 1974
26 Alice Munro to Buckler, 17 November 1973
27 Marian Engel to Buckler, 17 December 1974
28 Al Purdy to Buckler, 25 September 1967
29 Alister MacLeod to Buckler, 20 August 1970
30 Buckler to Barbara Hutchinson, 14 May 1969
31 Buckler to Bissell, 22 December 1972
32 Buckler to Margaret Laurence, 10 June 1974
33 Laurence to Buckler, 3 October 1974
34 Buckler to Laurence, 25 April 1975
35 Laurence to Buckler, 3 November 1974

CHAPTER SEVEN: LAST YEARS

1 Harold Brown to Buckler, 3 January 1969
2 Brown to Buckler, 21 September 1969
3 Buckler to Joan and Al McGuire and Rachel Grover, 29 May 1973
4 Jack McClelland to Buckler, 20 October 1967
5 Buckler to Farmer, 14 October 1971
6 Buckler to Farmer, 4 April 1973
7 Buckler to Farmer, 25 June 1974
8 Buckler to Bissell, 1 October 1975
9 Buckler to Bissell, 10 July 1974
10 Buckler to Laurence, 25 March 1976
11 Buckler to Bissell, 16 August 1980
12 *Ox Bells and Fireflies*, 110

A Bibliographical Note

There are two main sources of archival material for Buckler's life. Almost 90 per cent of it is in the Thomas Fisher Rare Book Library at the University of Toronto and the remainder is in the Public Archives of Nova Scotia in Halifax. The Toronto material consists of 34 boxes. The first 27 are arranged chronologically and contain drafts and typescripts of Buckler's writings and books, accompanied by correspondence relating to the particular work. Box 25 contains two MA theses and student papers about Buckler. Boxes 29 to 34 contain personal correspondence. My own correspondence with Buckler – around 200 letters – is the main group of letters. Buckler stipulated that the material in boxes 29 to 34 was not to be available to readers during his lifetime and, after his death, only with my permission.

The material in the Public Archives of Nova Scotia consists of a late diary beginning in 1952, which is meagre and factual. The collection adds substantially to the correspondence between Buckler and Margaret Bickley Farmer (boxes 2504 to 2508) and between Buckler and Evelyn Garbary (boxes 2500 to 2503). In both instances most of the letters are to Buckler. During the writing of this book, Mrs Farmer and Mrs Garbary made available to me Buckler's letters to them, and these letters have been deposited in the Toronto collection.

The books in the Buckler bibliography are as follows:
The Mountain and the Valley. New York: Henry Holt 1952;

Toronto: Clarke Irwin 1952; New York: New American Library
1954; Toronto: McClelland and Stewart, New Canadian Library
1961

The Cruelest Month. Toronto: McClelland and Stewart 1963; 1977

Ox Bells and Fireflies: A Memoir. New York: Knopf 1968;
Toronto: McClelland and Stewart 1968; Toronto: McClelland
and Stewart, New Canadian Library 1974

The Rebellion of Young David and Other Stories. Edited by Robert
Chambers. Toronto: McClelland and Stewart 1975

Nova Scotia: Window on the Sea. Toronto: McClelland and
Stewart 1973

Whirligig. Toronto: McClelland and Stewart 1977

Quotations from *The Mountain and the Valley*, *The Cruelest
Month*, and *Ox Bells and Fireflies* are from the New Canadian
Library edition of McClelland and Stewart.

Index